ARTS & CRAFTS FURNITURE

ARTS & CRAFTS
FURNITURE

From Classic to Contemporary

Kevin P. Rodel and Jonathan Binzen

The Taunton Press
Inspiration for hands-on living®

 The Taunton Press
Inspiration for hands-on living®

The Taunton Press, Inc.,
63 South Main Street,
PO Box 5506,
Newtown, CT 06470-5506
e-mail: tp@taunton.com

Distributed by Publishers Group West

Editor: Erica Sanders-Foege
Jacket/cover design: David Bullen
Interior design and layout: David Bullen
Illustrator: Melanie Powell
Cover photographers: (front cover) Photo by Randy O'Rourke; front flap: Courtesy H. Blairman & Sons, Ltd.; (spine) Courtesy H. Blairman & Sons, Ltd.; (back cover clockwise from top left) Courtesy Roycroft Arts Museum, Boice Lydell, Photo by Randy O'Rourke; © Dennis Griggs; © V & A Picture Library, Victoria and Albert Museum; Photo by Randy O'Rourke; (back flap top to bottom) © Dennis Griggs; © Bill Binzen; © The Metropolitan Museum of Art, Purchase, Lila Acheson Wallace Gift, 1994

Library of Congress Cataloging-in-Publication Data

Rodel, Kevin P.
  Arts & crafts furniture : from classic to contemporary / Kevin P.
Rodel and Jonathan Binzen.
    p. cm.
  ISBN 1-56158-359-6
  1. Arts and crafts movement. 2. Furniture--History--19th century. 3.
Furniture--History--20th century. I. Title: Arts and crafts furniture.
II. Binzen, Jonathan. III. Title.
  NK2394.A77R63 2003
  749.2'04--dc21

                              2003008779

Printed in the United States of America
10 9 8 7 6 5 4 3 2 1

Acknowledgments

WE EXTEND OUR HEARTFELT thanks to the many individuals and institutions that shared with us their knowledge, their furniture, and their photographs. Thanks to: Karen Baca, Cheryl A. Bachand, Simon Biddulph, Mary Beth Blatner, Ted Bosley, Nicola Gordan Bowe, John Burrows, Christian G. Carron, David Cathers, Ann and Andre Chavez, Lynda Clark, Michael Clark and Jill Thomas-Clark, Dennis Conta, Edward S. Cook, Jr., Crabtree Farm, Craftsman Auctions, Anna Tobin D'Ambrosia, Robert Edwards, Chase Ewald, Michael Fitzsimmons, Jeff Franke, Denis Gallion and Daniel Morris, Terry Geiser, Mary Greensted, Eric Hanson, Tim Hanson, Paula Healy, David Hellman, Denise Hice, Warren Hile, James Ipekjian, Lee Jester, Jennifer Komar-Olivarez, Kelmscott Manor, Stephen Lamont, Michael Levitin and Meredith Wise Mendes, John Alexander Levitties, Martin Levy, Ned Lipford, Boice Lydell, Randell Makinson, Mary Ann Meyers, Mr. and Mrs. Alexander Moser, Kathy Murphy, Janice McDuffie, Michael McGlynn, Beth Ann McPherson, Rago Auctions, Pamela Robertson, David Rudd, Suzanne Silkin, The L. & J. G. Stickley Co., David Stowe, Jennifer Strauss, The Swedenborgian Church of San Francisco, John Toomey, Peter Trowles, Kitty Turgeon, Frank D. Vagnone, Christopher Vickers, Rose Mary Watts, Eric Wildrick, Mark Willcox, Jr., Winterthur Library, Wright Auctions, and Debey Zito and Terry Schmitt.

To our primary photographer, Randy O'Rourke, our thanks for a fine job of capturing Arts and Crafts furniture on film. And kudos to Wendi Mijal for helping obtain and keep track of the hundreds of photos and permissions. To our editors at The Taunton Press, Helen Albert, Carolyn Mandarano, Erica Sanders-Foege, Diane Sinitsky, and Marilyn Zelinsky-Syarto, thanks for your excellent work and great perseverance on a long and complicated project. Our gratitude goes out to David Bullen for his superb design and layout for the book and its cover. Thanks also to Paula Schlosser and Rosalind Wanke for their skillful art direction. And to Jennifer Peters for keeping the project on track.

From Kevin Rodel: A very special thanks to longtime friends and mentors who opened my eyes to the many facets of Arts and Crafts design: David Berman, Bruce Smith, and Yoshiko Yamamoto.

And from Jonathan Binzen: My affectionate thanks to Karin Antonini, Annette Carruthers, Neville Neal, and Robert Smith Dods, who, perhaps unwittingly, sparked my interest in the English roots of Arts and Crafts furniture.

FOR MOM AND DAD
AND FOR CAROL
J.B.

FOR MY SONS,
RYAN AND JAMIE
K.P.R

Contents

Introduction

IN 1972, ROBERT JUDSON CLARK, a professor of art at Princeton University, curated an exhibition and edited an accompanying catalog that shook the Arts and Crafts movement from a 60-year slumber. In its salad days—roughly 1888 to 1910—the Arts and Crafts movement was a vibrant artistic, social, and philosophical phenomenon of international scope. But when the end of the era arrived, it was sudden and seemingly irreversible.

The Arts and Crafts movement was forward-looking in many ways—vitally concerned with the welfare of workers and with the integration of all forms of art—but it also yearned for a return to a preindustrial age of careful handcraftsmanship.

With the rise of the Bauhaus-bred International Style in architecture and design, which envisioned a future brightened by technology and an art stripped of all evidence of the past, the Arts and Crafts movement was brushed aside and made to seem utterly irrelevant. For many years, it was.

Since the Princeton show, however, hundreds of books and thousands of articles and essays have been written on Arts and Crafts topics; scores of exhibitions have been held; the value of Arts and Crafts furniture and other objects has increased enormously; and a revival of the style—and the lifestyle—has blossomed among craftsmen in a range of media.

The timing of this resurgence of interest in the Arts and Crafts movement is telling—it coincides with a wider revitalization of crafts in the United States. Only a small fraction of contemporary crafts are made in the Arts and Crafts style, but the revival as a whole—which rose out of the disaffection with established career paths and lifestyles in the 1960s and 1970s—is in many ways an exact parallel with the Arts and Crafts era, the original back-to-the-land movement.

In another echo of the original movement, major American furniture manufacturers have again embraced the style as they did during the Arts and Crafts movement's first flourishing. Today you can find Stickleyesque furniture in every department store and Sunday supplement. Despite the wide exposure, Arts and Crafts furniture remains largely misunderstood in the United States. For many, Stickley and his powerful, reductivist furniture stand for the whole broad movement.

But the Arts and Crafts movement refuses to be boiled down to one or two—or ten—signature pieces. The Arts and Crafts furniture produced in Vienna, Glasgow, and Pasadena was as different as strudel, haggis, and tacos. Our main purpose in writing this book is to present the entire spectrum of Arts and Crafts furniture so that we might better understand the movement's diversity and its originality.

Furniture of the Arts and Crafts Movement

CHIPPENDALE. SHAKER. Danish Modern. Many of the great furniture styles of the past have visual signatures that are as easily identified as their names. But this is not true of Arts and Crafts. The many designers aligned with the Arts and Crafts movement, whether working in London or Vienna, Glasgow or Brisbane, Stockholm or Syracuse, Chicago or San Francisco, shared design principles and philosophic approaches, but they created furniture that was extremely diverse in style.

Today in the United States, the furniture of Gustav Stickley dominates public perception of Arts and Crafts design. It's straight-lined, flat-planed, unembellished furniture that stands for solid earnestness. In England, the Cotswolds strain, with its rough detailing, prominent hand-joinery and humble forms, looms largest in retrospect. But each of these constitutes just one band in a broad spectrum of styles that comprised the Arts and Crafts movement.

Considering the movement's geographic reach, it's not surprising that a monolithic Arts and Crafts style doesn't exist. The Arts and Crafts movement—both a social and design revolution that took root in response to English industrializtion—quickly spread to Europe and the United States. Designers, architects, and critics were united in their protest against the effects of mechanization on the quality of life and on the quality of the resulting mass-produced goods. The prevailing Victorian aesthetic—deemed rigid and overly ornate—was roundly rejected in favor of freedom of expression.

From its beginnings, the movement was, in part, an attempt to reinvigorate craft traditions and to unify the decorative arts with their more privileged cousins, the fine arts. Although each of the decorative arts was represented in the movement, this book focuses on just the furniture—in all its great breadth and variety.

Social Reform, Design Revolution

The Arts and Crafts movement was christened in England in the late 1880s. But if its great exemplar, William Morris, had not shifted his studies from the clergy to the arts in his days at Oxford 35 years earlier, then what was to become known as the Arts and Crafts movement might not have happened at all.

Morris, born in 1834, was a member of the privileged class that transformed England from a rural and agrarian society to an urban and industrialized one. In this rapidly changing world, factories and mechanized mass production pushed aside traditional workshops and handcraftsmanship. Men like Morris, fired by the writings of art critic and social commentator John Ruskin, saw the results of industrialization as disastrous: Working conditions were, at best, undignified, while poorly designed and hastily made goods were flooding the market. Morris would dedicate his career to challenging the status quo in the arts and in the workplace.

William Morris was a gifted poet, novelist, linguist, and designer who spent much of his adult life working with his hands—weaving rugs and tapestry, mixing dyes—and reviving centuries-old craft traditions. He articulated and embodied the movement's ideals, blending manual and cerebral pursuits, living as he preached.

"No one can teach you anything worth learning but through manual labor. . . ."
John Ruskin, 1877

English Architects

The Arts and Crafts movement in England was largely one of architects, nearly all of whom trained in London and were deeply influenced by William Morris. His career was so encompassing that most of the designers of the movement eventually advanced one aspect or another of Morris's concerns.

The integrated interior—one in which everything from the architecture to the furniture and the floor coverings were designed by one hand in a unified language—was an idea central to the Arts and Crafts movement. It's demonstrated here in an interior by Leonard Wyburd which appeared in the 1907 *Studio Yearbook*.

C. R. Ashbee was among the English architects interested in exploring the social dimension of Morris's agenda. Ashbee's Guild and School of Handicraft trained working-class men in refined traditional craftsmanship. Although Ashbee gained reknown as a designer of furniture, metalwork, and jewelry, his primary interest lay in achieving social change.

Others of Morris's philosophical offspring sought to embody the ideal of the noble craftsman—the melding of designer and workman that Ruskin and Morris advocated. Sidney Barnsley, in particular, exemplified this path. Leaving London for the sleepy, still-unindustrialized Cotswolds region in the early 1890s, he spent his career designing and making furniture in a one-man shop.

One of the most influential and enduring ideas of the Arts and Crafts movement was Morris's conviction that a house and all its contents could be a wholly integrated work of art, which he illustrated clearly in his own Red House. This concept cut across geographic and stylistic boundaries. Several English Arts and Crafts architects, most

This is the original Morris chair, but it was not designed by Morris. Produced in 1865 by Morris & Co., it was adapted from a traditional chair by Morris's primary designer, Philip Webb.

Sidney Barnsley's approach to furniture making was among the most uncompromising of the Arts and Crafts era. He worked alone using only hand tools and built every piece he designed.

C. R. Mackintosh's 1904 washstand, with its rectilinearity and straightforward construction, incorporates elements of Arts and Crafts design. The use of other crafts—in this case tile and leaded glass—is also typical of Arts and Crafts furniture. The imagery in the leaded glass, however, with its hint of Art Nouveau, is distinctly different.

© The Metropolitan Museum of Art, Purchase , Lila Acheson Wallace Gift, 1994.
Photo © 1994 The Metropolitan Museum of Art

Austrian architects and designers were deeply influenced by the ideas of the English Arts and Crafts movement, but their work often showed distinct stylistic departures. This ebonized vitrine by Josef Hoffmann represents a new direction for Arts and Crafts ideas.

Courtesy © 2002, Historical Designs, Inc., N.Y.

notably C. F. A. Voysey and M. H. Baillie Scott, built their careers around the idea, designing for a wide range of craft media and providing their houses with everything from furniture to cutlery in a unified design language.

Scotland and Continental Europe

Outside of England, the social dimension of the movement was usually tempered with pragmatism.

In Scotland, architect and designer C. R. Mackintosh was influenced by Morris's concept of the house as a unified work of art, but he took little interest in the movement's concerns for the work life of the craftsman. And although Arts and Crafts elements are evident in his furniture, he showed a strong aesthetic independence that has led some furniture historians to link him to Art Nouveau or the Modern movement.

Arts and Crafts ideas took root across Scandinavia and Northern Europe, showing particular vigor in Germany and Austria. In Vienna, Josef Hoffmann focused on craftsmanship and the benefits of a humane workshop. But Hoffmann's mature style departed markedly from the aesthetics of English Arts and Crafts design. Hoffmann replaced the warmth of wood with opaque painted finishes. Eschewing country forms and tactile detailing, he explored a hard-edged, minimalist geometric style that prefigured the machine aesthetic of the Bauhaus and Modernism.

Another tenet of the Arts and Crafts movement was the desire for affordable decorative art. In Germany, this call was answered by designers in a range of *werkstatten,* or workshops, set up in line with Ruskin's philosophy. But to deliver on the promise of broadly accessible furniture, the German shops employed techniques of mass production, thereby compromising the English ideal of providing handmade goods.

Some of the most admired American Arts and Crafts furniture was made by brothers Charles and Henry Greene in Pasadena, California. Although the Greenes' furniture was influenced by Gustav Stickley, it was thoroughly reimagined with sensuous detailing and near-perfect execution.

Arts and Crafts in the United States

American designers embraced the Arts and Crafts movement with varied and far-reaching results. American furniture makers had been taking their stylistic cues from England since colonial days, and the Arts and Crafts movement was no excep-

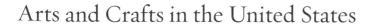

WHICH IS IT? ARTS AND CRAFTS, MISSION, OR CRAFTSMAN?

THE TERMS Mission, Craftsman, and Arts and Crafts are often mistakenly used interchangeably. In fact, they have quite distinct meanings.

Arts and Crafts is the umbrella term that applies generally to all crafts—from tiles and textiles to ceramics, furniture, and illuminated manuscripts—produced under the influence of anti-industrialist ideas for social reform. The ideas were first articulated by John Ruskin and William Morris. The term Arts and Crafts was coined after the Arts and Crafts Exhibition of 1888 in London. The movement, which emphasized handcraftsmanship, honest design, and local materials, began in England, then spread to continental Europe and America.

Mission refers generally to rectilinear American furniture of the Arts and Crafts movement. The term was apparently coined with reference to the simple, solid furniture of some Spanish missions in California. It's believed to have been first applied to work by Joseph McHugh but was subsequently adopted almost universally in the marketing campaigns of major American furniture manufacturers. Much of this furniture was originally inspired by Gustav Stickley's Craftsman line of furniture.

Craftsman is the trade name Stickley chose for his line of Arts and Crafts furniture. Although much American-manufactured furniture was made in imitation of Stickley's Craftsman line, none but Stickley's is properly called Craftsman furniture.

tion. The principles and rhetoric of the movement were adopted by a wide range of American designers—from small shops to large manufacturers.

Idealistic Americans formed utopian communities and cooperative workshops across the country. These ranged in hue from the purist—for example, William Price's Rose Valley outside Philadelphia—to the pragmatic, such as Elbert Hubbard's Roycroft community in upstate New York.

Other American designers, such as brothers Charles and Henry Greene in California and Charles Rohlfs in Buffalo, New York, made furniture notable for its rich blend of creativity and craftsmanship, which reached beyond English Arts and Crafts to embrace Asian and continental design concepts.

American designers also adopted the movement's integrated approach to whole-house design. Frank Lloyd Wright and his architect colleagues in the Prairie School designed houses and all their interior fittings and furnishings. Wright embraced many other aspects of Arts and Crafts philosophy, but he deviated sharply on the issue of hand craftsmanship. He openly challenged the Arts and Crafts' resistance to mechanization in his designs, which explicitly called for the use of machines.

Gustav Stickley's sideboard defines the Arts and Crafts style at its most rigid.

The broadest impact of the Arts and Crafts movement in American furniture was through large manufacturers. Beginning with Gustav Stickley's company, Craftsman Workshops, in 1901, one furniture manufacturer after another created product lines based on Arts and Crafts styles from England, Scotland, and continental Europe. With their marketing muscle and nationwide distribution, these companies gave the American brand of Arts and Crafts furniture a popular success the style never achieved in England.

Stickley's Craftsman Workshops espoused the philosophy of the movement and adapted its style. But to the majority of large companies, Arts and Crafts was simply one line of furniture among many. Advertising copy might be written to reflect the ideals of the movement, but the furniture was often no different than the mass-produced goods whose poor quality had catalyzed the movement to begin with.

Hallmarks of the Arts and Crafts Style

Designing for Morris & Co. in a style that shared little with that of Stickley, George Washington Jack produced some of the most elegant and refined furniture of the Arts and Crafts movement.

Taken as a whole, the furniture of the Arts and Crafts movement is not only diverse but also contradictory. Although the movement is best known for pieces that emphasize simplicity, solidity, and straight lines, it also produced works of refined proportions, sinuous lines, and complex ornamentation.

This duality was integral to Morris's philosophy of furniture design, which divided furniture between everyday pieces, which he advised should be of the simplest possible detailing, and formal pieces, which should be richly embellished.

Form

Arts and Crafts furniture speaks a language of morality. Designers eschewed the popular, historical-revival styles in favor of straightforward forms that bespoke function with a certain sternness. Linear motifs and flat planes, with their ring of the forthright, came to dominate the palette of many designers, beginning with English designer Ford Madox Brown's chunky furniture for Morris & Co. From Hoffmann in Vienna to Greene and Greene in California, a penchant for rectilinear forms suffused the movement.

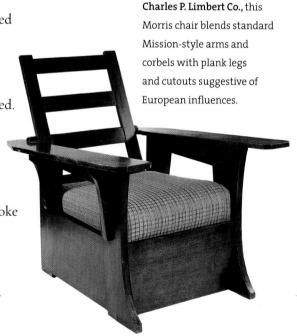

Made in Michigan by the Charles P. Limbert Co., this Morris chair blends standard Mission-style arms and corbels with plank legs and cutouts suggestive of European influences.

Strength, utility, and the noble craftsmanship of bygone days—Stickley designed his robust Craftsman furniture to stand for it all. Exposed joinery was often the only embellishment on his Craftsman pieces.

Yet George Washington Jack's furniture for Morris & Co. was highly refined and technically sophisticated. And William Price's Rose Valley furniture was derived directly from Gothic pieces and frequently featured extensive three-dimensional carving.

Joinery

In response to the increasing mechanization of furniture making, the Arts and Crafts movement expounded the importance of hand craftsmanship. To emphasize the point that a piece was made by skilled hands, many Arts and Crafts furniture designers produced furniture with exposed joinery—often the primary embellishment of the piece. Sidney Barnsley's painstakingly crafted dovetails were his attempt to keep craft traditions alive. Stickley, however, mindful of the bottom line but determined to make stout furniture, manufactured his through mortise-and-tenon joints by machine.

Exposed joinery was common in American Arts and Crafts furniture. But across the Atlantic, Voysey, Mackintosh, Hoffmann, and Morris & Co. most often made furniture with hidden mortise-and-tenon construction, which was more in keeping with a centuries-old trend toward concealing signs of workmanship.

Rough detailing—more evidence of handwork—was used on some Arts and Crafts furniture. This chest of drawers by Sidney Barnsley uses simple pattern carving to achieve a powerful feeling of directness.

Craftsmanship

A desire to reinvigorate craft traditions and techniques was at the heart of the Arts and Crafts movement. Ironically, in spite of the often-cited Arts and Crafts bias against machine use, most of the furniture was constructed with the help of machines. Designers were ambivalent on the topic. For all but the most fanatical of them, the goal was not to exclude the use of machines altogether but to keep the craftsman from becoming a factory worker—a mere feeder of machines.

Still, the idea of handwork exerted a powerful influence on makers and customers alike. From the smallest shops to the largest, Arts and Crafts furniture makers chose forms and

New York City furniture manufacturer, Joseph McHugh, sold a Morris chair embellished with a branching motif reminiscent of Tudor half-timbering.

details that denoted handwork. For the Cotswolds furniture makers, this meant leaving plane marks on the surfaces of tables or knife marks on carved drawer handles. For some large manufacturers, the impression of hand-craftsmanship was as important as the craftsmanship itself. Joseph McHugh, in New York City, produced furniture that sported ersatz exposed joinery while relying on hidden machine-cut joints to hold the pieces together.

Materials

Ruskin preached that the only honest and appropriate style was one that arose from local conditions and traditions. Accordingly, the Arts and Crafts movement embraced the use of domestic timbers rather than exotic ones. Stout, humble species such as oak and ash were favored among furniture makers on both sides of the Atlantic. The pronounced, open grain of these woods provided a corollary to the directness and integrity with which Arts and Crafts makers hoped to imbue their work. American designers showed a particular propensity for quartersawn oak with its prominent flecked figure.

Most Arts and Crafts furniture made use of local timbers in solid form as another way to express a lack of pretense. Of course, there were significant exceptions. Morris & Co. produced furniture that employed veneers and exotic woods. Ernest Gimson made many cabinets embellished with elaborate marquetry in ebony and other rare woods.

Custom-designed and handmade hardware was common on Arts and Crafts furniture. Designers also incorporated custom-made tiles, glass, fabrics, and leatherwork.

The Arts and Crafts movement reinvigorated a wide range of traditional crafts, and furniture of the time often incorporated work in other media. This folding screen by the Glasgow firm Wylie and Lochhead employs inlays of silver, mother-of-pearl, and turquoise as well as a pen-and-ink center panel by the artist Jessie King.

Designer David Kendall of Grand Rapids, Michigan, introduced a range of tinted finishes that were adopted by many producers of American Arts and Crafts furniture.

This heavyset Morris chair was built at Roycroft, Elbert Hubbard's quasi-utopian Arts and Crafts company in upstate New York. The chair embodies the community's straightforward furniture aesthetic.

Finishes

For Arts and Crafts designers who relished the appropriate and undisguised use of wood, clear finishes were the obvious and popular choice.

Some English and American designers did apply stains, and a light green wash became popular. Furniture manufacturers in Grand Rapids, Michigan, used a variety of stains. Fuming with ammonia, a process that darkens wood, also was a fairly common practice among large American Arts and Crafts manufacturers. But even when such color treatments were applied, they were generally followed with a transparent oil or varnish finish so that the grain of the wood remained visible.

Only a few Arts and Crafts furniture makers—most significantly Mackintosh and Hoffmann—used opaque finishes to obscure the wood grain. Both Mackintosh and Hoffmann produced pieces in pure black and others in stark white. Employed to increase the graphic impact of a piece, opaque finishes marked a radical departure from the familiar Arts and Crafts aesthetic, which valued wood for its natural qualities.

How the Movement Spread

The Arts and Crafts movement evolved through words as well as images. The bible of the movement was not a pattern book, as it had been for previous styles like Sheraton or Chippendale, but a book of social and art criticism, Ruskin's *Stones of Venice,* published in 1853. New technologies meant more people had access to information about the movement. The printed word, lectures, exhibitions, and magazine photographs all contributed to spreading the word.

C. R. Mackintosh was one of the few designers of Arts and Crafts-influenced furniture who used opaque finishes. He painted some pieces pure white, others black.

Magazines with a Message

Magazines delivered the news of the Arts and Crafts movement. With the invention of the photogravure printing process in the late 19th century, magazines began publishing printed photographs. Previously, images had to be laboriously made into engravings to be printed. The process instantly tightened the international circle, bringing clear images of new Glaswegian furniture to readers in Minnesota.

The Studio, a monthly magazine launched in London in 1893, did a thorough job of covering every aspect of the Arts and Crafts movement. Giving space to painting, architecture, and the decorative arts, *The Studio* was an embodiment of the movement's cherished ideal of unity among the fine and decorative arts.

The Studio was read avidly across Europe and in the United States. A special edition called *International Studio,* which included a supplement on the American scene, was published in the United States beginning in 1897.

In America, general-circulation magazines such as *House and Garden* and *Ladies' Home Journal* gave the movement signifi-

Launched in London in 1893, *The Studio* magazine, with its extensive coverage of Arts and Crafts architects, designers, and makers, was critical to the growth of the movement. An American edition, *International Studio,* contained a supplement on developments in the Arts and Crafts scene in the States.

Stickley's magazine, **The Craftsman,** presented the most comprehensive coverage of the American Arts and Crafts movement.

cant attention, introducing its ideas and aesthetic to a wide readership. As a result, the Arts and Crafts movement developed a broad constituency that included housewives and businessmen.

Stickley's New York-based magazine, *The Craftsman,* published from 1901 to 1915, developed a relatively modest circulation of some 20,000, but it was the clearest and most forceful voice of American Arts and Crafts style. Leading architects, artists, and designers of the day not only read the magazine but also wrote for it. *The Craftsman* championed the work of Arts and Crafts designers of all sorts. Carrying essays on the principles of the Arts and Crafts movement as well as detailed how-to articles on building furniture or designing a house, *The Craftsman* expressed the holistic spirit of the movement.

Elbert Hubbard brought the Arts and Crafts message to a far larger readership in his magazines, *The Fra* and *The Philistine.* With a blend of populist showmanship, self-promotion, and self-help that proved beguiling to hundreds of thousands of readers, Hubbard's magazines—like his communal company, Roycroft—managed to mix humble crafts with unrestrained capitalism.

The cerebral side of the movement was represented in the pages of small magazines such as *The Artsman,* the journal published by Price's utopian community at Rose Valley, Pennsylvania, and filled with closely argued essays on the origins and principles of the Arts and Crafts movement.

Word of Mouth on Stage

William Price, founder of the utopian Arts and Crafts community at Rose Valley, Pennsylvania, designed this Morris chair in his customary Gothic manner.

Word of the Arts and Crafts movement traveled quickly along the lecture circuit, which was another common and effective means of conveying ideas and information in the late 19th century.

Morris lectured extensively, spreading the reform message throughout England and to Scotland, where he spoke at the Glasgow School of Art while Mackintosh was a student there.

Speakers from Oscar Wilde to Ashbee brought Arts and Crafts ideas to lecture halls in America. Wilde, although more closely associated with the Aesthetic movement of the 1870s and '80s, spoke about home design in a way that fit the Arts and Crafts aesthetic. Ashbee, who made several lecture tours of the United States, befriended Frank Lloyd Wright on a visit to

Chicago in 1897 and the two argued the issue of handwork versus machinery. Hubbard lectured widely, too, spending months at a time on the road. His Roycroft campus was host to a constant stream of speakers.

Exhibitionism

Exhibitions large and small provided a third important avenue for disseminating the Arts and Crafts style and philosophy. Beginning with the Crystal Palace Exposition held in London in 1851, international trade and culture fairs became an enormous force in the global exchange of ideas, inventions, arts, customs, and crafts for more than half a century.

For American Arts and Crafts, the most important fair was the Louisiana Purchase Exposition held in St. Louis in 1904. Designers from around the world sent furniture to the show, and people made long pilgrimages to see it. Greene and Greene made the trek from California, Wright trained down from Chicago, and Charles Rohlfs made the trip from Buffalo, New York.

Exhibitions focusing on art and the decorative arts were numerous and of prime importance in introducing people to the latest Arts and Crafts work. Among the most influential were the seminal shows put on every few years from 1888 to 1916 by the Arts and Crafts Exhibition Society in London, the 1901 exhibition in Glasgow, and the 1902 exhibition in Turin, Italy, where works by Mackintosh and Rohlfs were an international success.

Josef Hoffmann's ebonized Morris chair, the *Sitzmachine,* demonstrates his affection for geometric forms.

"A book is a tool, for it is the instrument we make use of in certain cases when we wish to find out what other men have thought and done. . . . It is also true that a tool is a book, the record of past ages of talent engaged in toil."

D. C. Gilman, 1886

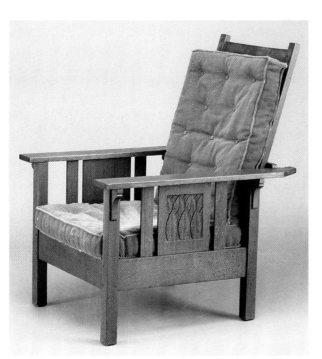

Morris chairs were made for the masses at such firms as L. & J.G. Stickley, which made this version. Like much of the company's work, it bears a close resemblance to Gustov Stickley's Craftsman furniture.

William Morris

The Roots of Arts and Crafts

WILLIAM MORRIS personally designed only four pieces of furniture, yet his impact on the furniture makers of the Arts and Crafts movement was profound. No other designer was able to approach the breadth and depth of his influence. Arts and Crafts furniture designers from Vienna to San Francisco cited Morris as their chief inspiration. He was embraced with equal fervor by utopians and industrialists, antiquarians and modernists. Frank Lloyd Wright, usually parsimonious with praise, said, "All artists love William Morris."

Morris's stature stemmed from an extraordinary blend of genius. He was a brilliant designer of decorative patterns, creating scores of designs for wallpaper, weavings, stained glass, and books. And in each of these fields he proved to be a gifted craftsman. Morris was also a popular and respected poet, a persuasive essayist and lecturer, and a political activist. It was not simply the number of his talents but the way they were blended that made him such a powerful inspiration for the generation that followed him.

One potent symbol of his ubiquitous influence is the Morris chair. Nearly every Arts and Crafts furniture maker—from individual craftsmen to mass manufacturers—made a version of the Morris chair. Making that chair was a rite of passage—and usually a sound business decision as well. Oddly, although it came to bear his name, the Morris chair, like the rest of the furniture produced by Morris & Co., was not designed by Morris, who left furniture design to others at his firm. It hardly mattered, though; what attracted so many to the chair was not so much its aesthetic appeal as its association with Morris, the progenitor of the Arts and Crafts movement.

The medieval temperament of Morris, Marshall, Faulkner & Co. is expressed in its St. George's cabinet, one of the firm's first pieces of furniture. Made in 1861 of mahogany, pine, and oak, it was designed by Philip Webb and painted by Morris with scenes depicting the legend of St. George.

William Morris, an artist, poet, craftsman, and the soul of the Arts and Crafts movement, made this self-portrait in 1865, when he was 31.

Furnishing the Red House

In 1859, three years after graduating from Oxford, William Morris asked his friend, Philip Webb, an architect, to design him a house in a small town outside of London. Built from bricks made of ruddy local clay, the building earned the name Red House. Over the course of the next two years, Morris and Webb and a cluster of their artistic friends—including the Pre-Raphaelite painters Dante Gabriel Rossetti and Ford Madox Brown, as well as painter Edward Burne-Jones—set about designing and creating nearly every object that would furnish the house, including stained-glass windows, wall-hung tapestries, frescoes, murals, and embroidery.

In the process of furnishing Red House, the spirited group set a number of precedents that would reverberate through the decorative arts world in the succeeding half-century. To begin with, the project stemmed from a wholesale rejection of the furnishings available for purchase at the time. "Shoddy is king," Morris lamented, and he did not intend to have anything of poor quality in his house. Low-grade goods were, in part, a result of machine production. Morris insisted that Red House would be a paean to handcraftsmanship.

Red House was trendsetting, too, as a building whose exterior and interior were fully integrated, and whose furnishings were designed specifically for the site.

The furnishings of Red House were deeply imbued with a Gothic spirit, which would prove to be significant to the Arts and Crafts movement. The Gothic influence was explicit in Red House furniture, which was painted with scenes described in medieval literature. The experience of furnishing Red House led directly to the formation of Morris, Marshall, Faulkner & Co. (later Morris & Co.), which would inspire a range of artisan guilds and cooperatives in Europe and the United States.

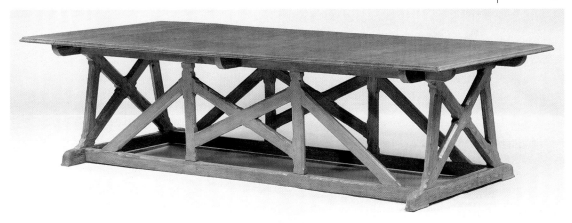

With unfussy pieces like this refectory table from about 1840, with its beautifully expressed structure, English architect A.W.N. Pugin prepared the way for the undecorated, Gothic-tinged furniture made by some in the Arts and Crafts movement.

A.W.N. PUGIN
(1812–1852)

Gothic Prodigy

English architect Augustus Welby North-more Pugin was largely responsible for the flowering of the Gothic revival in the early 1800s. Many of his ideas perfectly prefigure the principles of the Arts and Crafts movement. Pugin's output as a designer was prodigious, and he also wrote several influential books. Born in 1812, Pugin lived only 40 years, but he got an early start, providing designs for furnishings on his architect father's jobs—including work for the royal family—by the age of 15.

Pugin's outpouring of designs included many for the furnishings in his buildings. Some of his furniture designs were crowded with carvings, but others, reduced to little more than structure, stand as direct precursors of work by designers from Philip Webb to Gustav Stickley. John Ruskin, who'd once been accused of cribbing ideas from Pugin, denounced the architect's buildings as worthless. Ruskin's clout as a critic seems to have been sufficient to tarnish Pugin's reputation, which suffered for decades thereafter.

Morris & Co.:
A Guild Goes into Business

Morris, Marshall, Faulkner & Co., the collaborative founded in 1862 by a group of dreamers and idealists emulating the medieval guilds, did an unlikely thing: It managed to survive. From the start, the group attracted clients and critical notice. The firm took on comprehensive commissions to design and furnish houses, and built a retail business selling its own furnishings and fabrics.

The character of the firm's products would evolve as its principals matured, but an extraordinary level of quality existed from the beginning. A number of furniture and pattern designs that were introduced in the mid-1860s were still in production when the company finally closed its doors in 1940. By 1875, when Morris reorganized the company and renamed it Morris & Co., his patterns in fabric and wallpaper were known throughout Europe and the United States.

Morris had a great talent for textile design. Along with his superb patterns for wallpaper—many of which are still produced—he excelled in designing chintzes, carpets, and tapestries.

Morris's Furniture Designers

Chief among the company's furniture designers was Philip Webb. Also the firm's top architect, Webb was responsible for much of the furniture created to fill his houses. His designs ranged from large, stout medieval-inspired cabinets and settles to delicate, delightfully restrained tables and formal, richly inlaid cabinets.

The Victorian appetite for ostentatious ornament was fed by manufacturers who produced poorly copied historic revival furniture and concocted designs like this server.

Webb's protégé, the American-born and Scottish-bred George Washington Jack, helped with the firm's furniture design throughout the 1880s. When Webb retired, Jack assumed the central role of designing in 1890. Jack's designs would show some of the same delicacy as Webb's, but Jack concentrated increasingly on more elaborate case goods with a Queen Anne influence.

In the firm's first decade, the painter Ford Madox Brown contributed fascinating furniture designs that were heavy, unadorned, and extremely straightforward. More than anything else that the firm produced, Brown's designs provided a possible aesthetic inspiration for the stark, structural work of designers such as A. H. Mackmurdo in the 1880s and Gustav Stickley in the 1900s.

A Genius for Textiles

Throughout its eight-decade history, Morris & Co. was most noted for its textiles. The majority of the designs were from Morris's pen, including embroidery, chintzes, upholstery fabrics, carpets, and tapestries.

Textiles played a pivotal role in creating a Morris interior. Printed and woven patterns would combine and complement each other as carpets, draperies, and upholstery to form an integrated interior. This approach to design laid the foundation for the unified wood interiors created by Frank Lloyd Wright in the Midwest and by Greene and Greene in California.

Morris's first commercial print patterns debuted in 1862. Eventually he developed 144 known patterns. To design textiles, Morris often went back to original manuscripts describing methodologies and he revived lost practices, especially techniques for dyeing with plant extracts.

For Morris, a successful textile pattern was carefully pondered. He studied how the material would be used—as a wall covering,

Courtesy J.R. Burrows

upholstery fabric, or carpet—and considered the characteristics of the material. How a textile took color and how it lay, or draped, were weighed—silk, cotton, and wool all had their own properties that affected the success of a pattern. To Morris, "the special limitations of the material should be a pleasure to you, not a hindrance." Printed and woven patterns would combine and complement each other as carpets, draperies, and upholstery to form a unified interior of color and pattern.

> *"I do not want art for a few, any more than education for a few or freedom for a few."*
>
> William Morris, 1877

The designers responsible for the most influential—or at least the most enduring—of the firm's furniture designs remain essentially anonymous. While visiting small cabinet shops in Sussex in 1865, the firm's recently hired business manager, Warington Taylor, came across a chair that he thought the company should consider producing. He made a quick sketch of it and sent the rendering to Philip Webb. The reclining chair, which became known as the Morris chair, was soon for sale in the company's retail store. Another found country chair was the basis for the light, inexpensive piece the firm called the Sussex chair. Both chairs sold extremely well for the company and stayed in production until Morris & Co. closed.

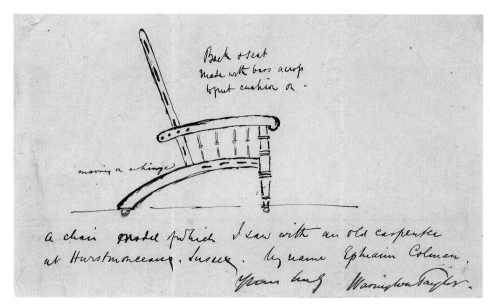

This quick sketch by Warington Taylor, the business manager of Morris, Marshall, Faulkner & Co., led to the design of the famous Morris chair. Taylor came across a simple chair in a cabinet shop and passed along his sketch of it to Philip Webb, who used it as the basis for the Morris chair.

IN DETAIL : WORKADAY AND STATE FURNITURE

> *"It is only by labor that thought can be made healthy, and only by thought that labor can be made happy, and the two cannot be separated with impunity."*
>
> John Ruskin, 1856

For William Morris, furniture design fell into two distinct categories: the simple, straightforward "workaday" or cottage furniture, and the more elaborately designed and technically challenging "state" furniture. To Morris's thinking, both design approaches were valid as long as they were rooted in the ideal of the craftsman as artist.

The simple, primitive Gothic round table shown below, attributed to Morris, exemplifies the idea of workaday furniture.

The highly refined six-legged tea table by George Washington Jack (1888) shown below is an example of Morris's state furniture. The delicate, sensitively ornamented components speak well of the craftsman's art and skill. However, the many workaday furniture pieces developed by various English designers would make the greatest impression on American designers.

Members of the Arts and Crafts movement were not alone in producing designs that reacted against the excesses of Victorian design. This 1875 oak sideboard by George F. Roper, with its straightforward plank construction and Gothic cutouts, is a step toward simplification and the clear expression of function.

The Art of Morris & Co.

MORRIS & CO.'S FURNITURE ranged from the stark to the sophisticated. Morris himself designed no furniture for the firm, leaving that work to designers such as Philip Webb and George Washington Jack. But Morris's theory that everyday furniture should be basic and unadorned, whereas more formal pieces should be complex and highly embellished set the firm's course. Morris & Co.'s earliest designs were heavily influenced by Gothic furniture forms and were often painted with medieval scenes or floral patterns. Ford Madox Brown's furniture of the 1860s, with heavy timbers and wide chamfers painted in solid colors, set a standard for simplicity. Jack, who led the firm's furniture department in the 1890s, preferred slender forms and finely articulated details.

ONE OF MORRIS & CO.'S *most popular designs, the Sussex chair was in production from 1864 until 1940. The Sussex chair, although attributed to Ford Madox Brown, was essentially a copy of a traditional country chair.*

AN ARTS AND CRAFTS ICON, *the Morris chair was introduced in 1865 and became a staple in the Morris & Co. catalog for 75 years. Although named for Morris, it was designed by his friend Philip Webb who based it on a traditional English chair.*

MORRIS HAD JUST GRADUATED *from Oxford when he designed this chair, along with a mammoth settle and an extremely heavy table, for the London apartment he shared with Edward Burne-Jones. Morris's fascination with medieval furniture drove the design. The scenes on the chair back were painted by Pre-Raphaelite artist Dante Gabriel Rossetti.*

An example of what Morris would call workaday *furniture, this oak table was designed for Morris & Co. by Philip Webb in 1865. Webb created an interesting geometric interplay with its stretchers and introduced a hint of the exotic with faux-bamboo turnings.*

DESIGNED BY GEORGE WASHINGTON JACK
*in about 1890, this highly refined tea table is
among his more restrained pieces. Jack's work
was often more elaborate, employing extensive
stringing, inlay, and feats of cabinetmaking
prowess. Whether plain or fancy, Jack's work
was distinguished by a sensitive line and
pleasing proportions.*

THE GOTHIC ROOTS OF THE FIRM *are hard to see in this Georgian-influenced cabinet, designed by George Washington Jack in 1902. After Morris's death in 1896, Jack's designs shifted more clearly toward high-style period furniture forms.*

Arts and Crafts in the Country

Gimson, the Barnsleys, and the Cotswolds Vernacular

IN 1893, in the rural Cotswold hills of central England, Sidney Barnsley, his brother Ernest, and their friend Ernest Gimson set up a furniture workshop after apprenticing as architects in London. Inspired by William Morris, the three men sought to develop a style that incorporated the regional vernacular. Over the next three decades, they produced furniture that has become some of the most highly regarded of the Arts and Crafts movement and some truest to the movement's ideals.

When Sidney Barnsley displayed an oak buffet at the 1899 Arts and Crafts Exhibition, one critic called it "the work of a savage." Even viewed alongside hundreds of other objects inspired by the movement's call for simplicity and honesty in design, Barnsley's piece, with its radical roughness of detailing, had the power to shock. A century later, the buffet retains a raw vitality, but these days it seems less the work of a savage than of a savant.

In overall form, the buffet reveals the group's affinity for the direct, rugged shapes of English country case pieces. Its board-and-batten end doors, plank construction, and clear-finished oak also speak to the simplicity of country furniture. And the exposed joinery and carved door handles demonstrate that for Gimson and the Barnsleys, the vernacular was not just a matter of style but of technique.

In addition to producing a large body of work in this strong, country mode, the group—especially Gimson—designed a range of more urbane pieces, employing refined shapes, exotic veneers, and custom-designed silver hardware.

Against long odds, Gimson and the Barnsleys developed a vital style rooted in the dying crafts of the countryside. They went about it with a passion for craftsmanship; many who worked with them shared that passion and became noted designers and mentors in their own right.

A prime expression of Sidney Barnsley's deliberately unsophisticated style, this 1897 oak hutch makes use of the forms of country furniture and the techniques of traditional crafts. Barnsley's rugged work set the tone for the Cotswolds group.

London Calling

Gimson and the Barnsleys, who had grown up in the mid-sized cities of Leicester and Birmingham, were from well-to-do families. Like many English Arts and Crafts designers, they made their way to London in the late 1880s to become architects.

Gimson and Ernest Barnsley found work in the office of John Dando Sedding, while Sidney Barnsley was employed by Norman Shaw. Both were elite offices with close ties to William Morris—Sedding's was right next door to the Morris & Co. showroom on Oxford Street. Both offices would produce many stars of the Arts and Crafts movement.

It was a time of great ferment and excitement for those on the London architectural scene, and the three men received much of their education outside their offices. There were meetings of the Art Workers Guild, the Arts and Crafts

IN DETAIL : THE REBIRTH OF GUILDS

SOCIETIES AND GUILDS blossomed in London at a rate of one every two years through the 1880s. Inspired by medieval craft guilds, they all shared the goal of promoting handcraftsmanship and the decorative arts, as well as improving the working conditions of craft labor. The example of the English guilds spawned similar experiments abroad, from Josef Hoffmann's Wiener Werkstatte in Austria to the utopian craft communities of Roycroft, Byrdcliffe, and Rose Valley in the United States.

Morris & Co. 1862-1940
Design firm and retail company.
WIlliam Morris, Dante Gabriel Rosetti,
Philip Webb, Ford Madox Brown, Edward Burne-Jones

Century Guild 1882-1888
Affiliation of designers and craftsmen.
A.H. Mackmurdo, Selwyn Image

Art Worker's Guild, 1884 to present
Professional society of architects, designers, and craftsmen.
William R. Lethaby, Lewis F. Day, W.A.S. Benson

Arts & Crafts Exhibition Society 1886-1916
Organization devoted to mounting exhibitions; and offshoot of the
Art Workers Guild. Walter Crane, W.A.S Benson, T.J. Cobden-Sanderson

Guild of Handicrafts 1888-1910
Workshop producing fine crafts and training low-income men in
traditional techniques. C.R. Ashbee.

Kenton & Co. 1890-1892
Design collective sharing a common furniture workshop.
William Lethaby, Ernset Gimson, Ernest and Sidney Barnsley

Exhibition Society, and the Society for the Protection of Ancient Buildings—all groups established to advance the ideals articulated by John Ruskin and Morris, which were beginning to coalesce into the Arts and Crafts movement.

In 1890, Gimson and the Barnsleys, along with William Lethaby and several other architects, founded their own guildlike group, Kenton & Co. The idea was to form a loose collective of furniture designers who would share the costs of establishing a shop and hiring furniture makers. There would be no manifesto and no house style; each member would be free to design as he pleased. Kenton & Co. produced enough furniture to mount an exhibition, which drew positive notices. Unfortunately, it soon dissolved for lack of funding.

Designed by William Lethaby, a key member with Gimson and the Barnsleys of the Kenton & Co. cooperative, this sideboard draws on cottage furniture for inspiration. But with extensive inlays and finely joined arched galleries, its craftsmanship is far from rudimentary.

To the Cotswold Countryside

Ernest Gimson studied the techniques of his craft but remained a designer. Unlike his friend Sidney Barnsley, Gimson relied upon his craftsmen to execute his designs.

Gimson and the Barnsleys lacked the political passion that gripped many of their contemporaries in the movement. But if they weren't inspired to crusade for socialism, they did seek a social change for themselves. Gimson and the Barnsleys were enamored of the ideal of the countryside. Like many others in the movement, they felt that leaving the industrial centers was a step toward the richer life and the more rewarding work of the medieval past.

Following Morris's lead (whose country house, Kelmscott Manor, was in the nearby hamlet of Lechlade), the three found their way to the pastoral Cotswold countryside. With beautiful topography and an economy untouched by industrialization, the Cotswolds offered a nearly pristine way of life.

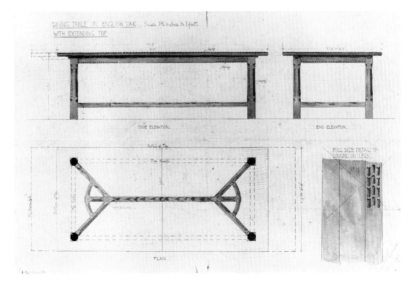

Sidney Barnsley's library table eschews all ornamentation, relying for its impact on the power of pure form. Made in 1920 for Gimson's Bedales School library, Barnsley's table echoes William Morris's belief that furniture ought to be made of "timber rather than walking sticks."

Settling into old stone buildings, the three young designers launched their second experiment in collective furniture making.

Sidney Barnsley: Raw Vernacular

Perhaps more than any other Arts and Crafts furniture maker, Sidney Barnsley embodied the movement's twin ideals of the designer immersed in craft and the craftsman attuned to design.

Barnsley's apprenticeship in London and sketching tours of the Continent provided him with a sophisticated knowledge of historical styles. When he arrived in the Cotswolds in 1893, he essentially abandoned architecture, reinventing himself as a designer and learning furniture making from the inside out as he struggled by trial and error to become a craftsman.

Barnsley produced the purest form of the Cotswolds furniture style. Following Morris's example, he learned his craft by making his furniture by hand. But unlike other Arts and Crafts designers, Barnsley never laid down his tools. As long as he was able, he crafted every piece that he designed.

Each piece expressed Barnsley's fidelity to function and his belief in the integrity of handcraftsmanship. From first to last, his work cleaved to elemental forms. It relied on vigorously expressed joinery and on details adapted from rural crafts for its ornamentation.

A traditional Cotswolds hay rake provided the design for the stretcher system on this Sidney Barnsley table in the Bedales library.

Along with his brother and Gimson, Barnsley learned woodworking by examining old pieces of furniture and consulting local craftsmen. The group also absorbed the structure and detailing of items such as wagons and farm implements: A number of Barnsley's tables, for instance, incorporate a Y-shaped stretcher system that is directly related to the sturdy, triangulated yoke of a common Cotswolds hay rake.

A typical Sidney Barnsley piece would be made of solid wood—normally oak, occasionally other local timbers—and would be of very sturdy proportions. To keep the heavy parts from appearing clunky, Barnsley would make them deeply chamfered, or beveled. Barnsley's joinery and structure were not simply exposed but emphasized: Through tenons protruded, dovetails stood proud, and stretchers, panels, and back slats could all serve as the focus of a piece. Tabletops were thick and made from two or three wide planks. Wood was not smoothed out with dulling sandpaper, but left instead with the clean-sliced, slightly irregular surface produced by a handplane, a drawknife, or a spokeshave.

Every piece of Barnsley's furniture was solidly functional. On pieces such as his buffet or his chip-carved bureau, the door and drawer pulls were shaped for an easy, sure grip and attracted the eye as well as the hand.

Barnsley was a solitary man by nature, and his pursuit of joy in his work always brought him back to the process of work itself. "The worker," Ruskin wrote, "ought often to be thinking, and the thinker often to be working." Barnsley lived Ruskin's ideal.

Handwork is at the heart of the Cotswolds style. The chip-carved door handles on Sidney Barnsley's hutch spell out his passion for the personal touch.

IN DETAIL : THE ART OF UTILITY

THE ARCHITECTURE and craft traditions of the Cotswolds were largely unchanged by England's rapid industrialization. Although the local architecture was almost exclusively limestone, the interior structures and decorations were solid, centuries-old timberwork.

The agriculture-based crafts of the wheelwright and wagon builder were done almost entirely by hand, creating forms and implements of pure utility. Gimson and the Barnsleys were quick to learn from this environment. Ernest Gimson's library at Bedales School reveals his love of the heavy timbers and the solid joinery of rural crafts, as well as his training as an architect in a time when the ultimate commission was a church. The chairs are by Gimson and the tables by Sidney Barnsley.

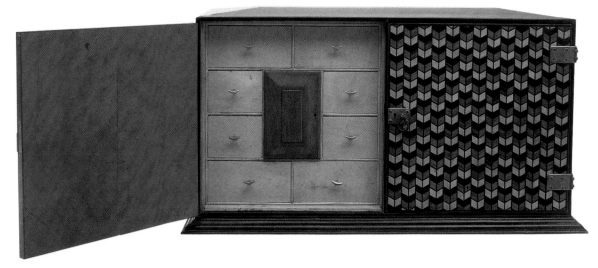

Ernest Gimson had an eye for the exquisite. This tabletop cabinet, inlaid with ebony, walnut, and holly, and fitted with custom-made silver pulls on whitebeam drawer fronts, is a compact expression of his sensibility at its most sophisticated.

Ernest Gimson: Elegant Vernacular

Ernest Gimson's Cotswolds furniture, while in some ways vitally connected to Sidney Barnsley's, is often strikingly different. Like Barnsley, Gimson drew heavily on the informal shaping and frank joinery of country woodcraft, but Gimson married these forms with more refined, urban influences. Whereas Barnsley worked strictly with solid wood in local species, Gimson often employed veneer and exotic woods. Although some of Gimson's designs spoke in the rough, humble forms of daily use, others—such as his sheer-sided showpieces decorated with geometric marquetry— utilized a more sophisticated, abstract vocabulary. And where

Gimson's oeuvre included unadorned, elemental pieces like this ebonized hutch. Even his most rudimentary furniture exhibited a preference for geometric form and an unerring sense of proportion.

This ladder-back is the work of Philip Clissett, a "badger" or green-wood chair maker. Using a foot-powered lathe, Clissett made chairs much admired by Gimson from the 1850s into the 1890s.

Barnsley made all his own pieces, Gimson used a small crew of skilled craftsmen to execute his designs.

The division in Gimson's work between highly polished, ornamented pieces and simpler, rougher ones is a direct reflection of the distinction Morris described between workaday and state furniture. Most furniture, Morris said, should be made purely for use, but the more prominent case pieces—sideboards, for example—ought to be made as elegantly as possible. Gimson's abundant gifts enabled him to design superb pieces on both sides of this divide.

Morris & Co. had enormous success with its Sussex and Morris chairs, both of which were closely based on traditional designs. Perhaps inspired by these unpretentious pieces, Gimson began making a traditional chair of his own after he met Philip Clissett in 1888.

Clissett was a "badger"—a man who made chairs from green wood—who had been making handsome ladder-backs since the 1850s. Gimson spent several weeks learning the craft from Clissett and was soon making chairs himself. Later, Gimson hired Edward Gardiner to make them. Over the next two decades, Gardiner and his helpers produced hundreds of chairs according to Gimson's Clissett-based designs.

Ernest Barnsley

When Gimson and the Barnsley brothers set up shop in the Cotswolds, all three made furniture. Gimson and Ernest Barnsley spent time in the workshop but continued to practice architecture as well. By 1899, the two decided to form a partnership devoted primarily to furniture making. They leased a larger workshop and hired craftsmen.

Ernest Barnsley designed a limited amount of furniture, most of it directly influenced by his brother Sidney's vernacular style. Within a few years, however, Ernest's relationship with Gimson soured, the partnership was dissolved, and Ernest Barnsley and his family moved from the Cotswolds. Gimson remained and redoubled his efforts in furniture design.

Gimson began making turned chairs after a brief apprenticeship with Clissett in the late 1880s. In this 1895 ladder-back, Gimson adopted all the essentials of Clissett's chair, refining the posts and rungs, and flattening the slats to achieve a design with more graphic bite.

The Cotswold Legacy

By 1910, across England and America, the popularity of the Arts and Crafts style was waning. Ten years later, few traces of the style were left. But in the Cotswolds, the style and its craftsmen showed impressive endurance.

Although Gimson died in 1919, his crew of craftsmen, led by the exceptionally talented Dutchman Peter van der Waals, stayed in business through the 1930s. Edward Gardiner, Gimson's chairmaker, continued to produce chairs using Gimson's patterns into the late 1950s.

Sidney Barnsley's son, Edward, was also instrumental in carrying on the Cotswolds tradition. Edward trained with a former craftsman of Gimson's and went on to become perhaps the finest English furnituremaker of his generation. Blending the simplicity of his father's furniture with the refined forms of Regency style, he continued the tradition of honest, unyielding craftsmanship.

C. R. Ashbee

Like Gimson and the Barnsleys, C. R. Ashbee was an Arts and Crafts designer who studied in London and eventually settled in the Cotswolds. Ashbee was as much a political and social activist as he was an artist. Inspired by Ruskin's writings, he founded the Guild and School of Handicraft in London's impoverished East End in 1888. The idea was to teach craft skills to working-class men while producing high-quality items to support the school.

Surprisingly, the idea worked. The Guild not only supported itself for the next 12 years but also gained wide recognition for the quality of its products. Along with Ashbee's designs for furniture, metalware, and jewelry, the Guild executed

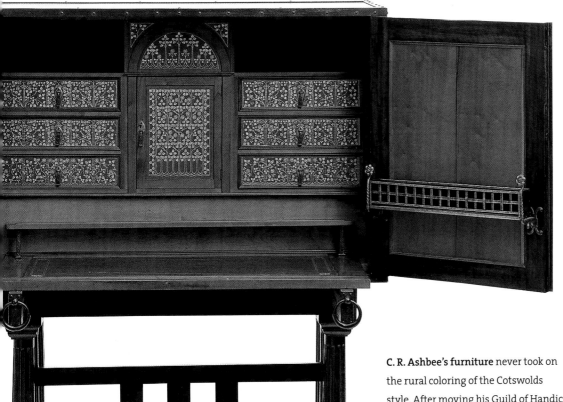

"If one's interest in the work were only that of design and utility, it would be different but it is in the men themselves too and their ways of work and through that to most things in life. . . ."

Ernest Gimson, 1900

C. R. Ashbee's furniture never took on the rural coloring of the Cotswolds style. After moving his Guild of Handicraft to the area from London in 1900, he continued to design highly ornamented pieces like this cabinet, which has its roots in medieval Spanish furniture.

designs by prominent Arts and Crafts designers such as Hugh Baillie Scott and C. F. A. Voysey.

In 1902, Ashbee decided to move the Guild to the Cotswolds. In the picturesque town of Chipping Campden, he found workspace in a former silk mill and leased various buildings for housing. Remarkably, some 70 craftsmen attached to the Guild relocated to the countryside with their families.

The Guild had its difficulties fitting in to the life of the small town. Eventually the transition was made and craft production resumed, but even this recovery was short-lived. The Guild closed in 1910.

Cotswolds Country

ERNEST GIMSON AND THE BROTHERS Ernest and
Sidney Barnsley moved to the rural Cotswolds from London
in the early 1890s determined to live the Arts and Crafts ideal
of the thinking craftsman. Together the three men developed
a vivid furniture style rooted in the traditional forms and
techniques of the region's crafts: wagons, hay rakes, barrels,
barns. They built with heavy timbers, linking them with
pegged, exposed joints and decorating them with the heavy
chamfering they saw on farm implements. The rudimentary
forms and traditional techniques were carefully considered.
The men had trained as architects, and even their most
elementary furniture displayed a sophisticated appreciation
of line, massing, and texture. Ernest Barnsley moved away
in the early 1900s, but Gimson and Sidney Barnsley stayed
on in the Cotswolds, producing furniture
for two more decades.

DELICATE CHIP CARVING *along the
top and legs introduces a few lines
of texture in Sidney Barnsley's massive
oak table of about 1923. The table's
muscular design is braced by the hay-
rake shaped stretcher, an element
he developed 25 years earlier.*

PROUD DOVETAILS AND THROUGH TENONS
*make Sidney Barnsley's blanket chest an essay in
exposed joinery. Built in the late 1890s, the chest is
also notable for its vigorous chamfering—a technique
used on farm implements to reduce an object's weight
without sacrificing strength.*

SIDNEY BARNSLEY

Sidney Barnsley was chiefly responsible for the rugged flavor of the Cotswolds style. Working alone and crafting his pieces himself throughout his career, he built furniture whose structure was clear and powerful. In all his pieces, function was the primary concern. Exposed joinery and expressed structure provided much of the visual interest, but the work was also embellished with bands of chip carving. Barnsley used mostly local woods in solid form and coated them with clear finishes.

MORE REFINED IN ITS PROPORTIONS *than most of
Barnsley's furniture, this oak couch from about 1920
is still based on pure utilitarian forms: The distinctive
pattern of the back is modeled after the ribbed-paneled
sides found on mid-19th-century farm wagons.*

ERNEST GIMSON

Ernest Gimson built some furniture in the raw Cotswolds style, but more often his pieces combined elements of the rural vernacular with elevated forms and rich decoration. The play of the formal and informal, the plain and the complex, the rough and the elegant supply a unique spirit to Gimson's best work. Adept at using the country forms but not confined to them, Gimson also designed pieces that show no hint of the Cotswolds style.

TYING TOWN AND COUNTRY TOGETHER, *Gimson's 1915 sideboard marries the proportions and rich materials of a formal sideboard with the heavy chamfers and arched framing of a farm wagon. Among Arts and Crafts furniture makers, only Gimson so successfully blended the high and low. Gimson's talented crew of craftsmen executed not only the impeccable woodworking in the piece but also cast the hardware.*

STRONG GEOMETRIC SHAPES
recur in Gimson's furniture. When
he strayed from the Cotswolds style,
Gimson moved toward abstraction.
This fall-front writing desk built
in 1904 presents an almost irre-
ducible form. Only the sled-foot
base keeps the piece from being
an entirely clean modern box.

MANY OF GIMSON'S DESIGNS
display a willingness to explore
beyond the Cotswolds vocabulary
that he had helped establish.
This china hutch from about 1901,
with a paper-thin overhanging
top, delicate glazing, and geometric
veneer patterns, is a radical departure from the rugged work Sidney
Barnsley was doing.

English Architects and Designers

Baillie Scott's innovative instrument—essentially an upright with the keyboard enclosed—came to be called the Manx piano because he lived on the Isle of Man. On this Manx, Baillie Scott's decorative bent gives way to a solid-wood surface with hammered strap hinges evocative of medieval weaponry.

THE IDEAS AND the energy that sparked and spread the Arts and Crafts movement in England were provided largely by architects. London architects rallied together in the 1880s, founding a series of guilds and associations that culminated in the Arts and Crafts Exhibition Society. These groups aimed to elevate architecture as well as the many crafts of the decorative arts—from plasterwork and stained glass to textiles, metalwork, and furniture—to the level of the fine arts.

Striving to forge this unity, Arts and Crafts architects began creating designs for various decorative arts as well as for buildings. A.W. N. Pugin, whose work served as a precursor to the movement, designed interior fittings and furniture expressly for his buildings in London in the 1830s and 1840s. The same idea was elaborated in William Morris's Red House of 1859, which was designed by Philip Webb and furnished down to the last dessert fork by Morris and his circle. C. F. A. Voysey and M. H. Baillie Scott excelled at designing relatively small houses and filling them with custom-made furnishings.

Voysey and Baillie Scott both produced furniture that represented the core Arts and Crafts ideal of clearly expressed structure. But unlike such purists as Sidney Barnsley, Voysey and Baillie Scott designed a wide range of products meant to be manufactured in large numbers and sold through retail stores.

England experienced nothing like the tidal wave of manufactured Arts and Crafts furniture that flooded the United States, but there was a healthy retail trade through several prominent stores such as Liberty & Co. and Heal & Son. Liberty & Co., in particular, commissioned work by many of the best designers associated with the movement and developed a hybrid style that achieved international influence.

A. H. Mackmurdo and the Awakening of Arts and Crafts

A. H. Mackmurdo's furniture output was small but potent. His 1886 desk, straight-lined and unembellished, prefigures Stickley's rectilinear Craftsman line.

Arthur Heygate Mackmurdo had a gift for beginnings. His career as an architect and designer was relatively short, but it produced a handful of extremely influential objects and endeavors.

Perhaps most prominent among Mackmurdo's successes was his desk of 1886. With its radical rectilinearity, its unadorned surfaces, and its architectural play of horizontal and vertical elements, it was a potent distillation of Arts and Crafts principles. And it provided the starting point for a style that would be carried forward by English Arts and Crafts designers such as C. F. A. Voysey and Americans such as Gustav Stickley and Elbert Hubbard.

Ironically, Mackmurdo was also responsible for a design that proved equally seminal for the furniture style that was the complete antithesis of Arts and Crafts. His poppy chair of about 1883, with its pierce-carved back of slender, sinuous flowers, was a clear precursor of the Art Nouveau style.

The Century Guild

In addition to his aesthetic impact, Mackmurdo exerted an important social influence on the Arts and Crafts movement. A student of Ruskin's at Oxford, Mackmurdo adopted his teacher's views on the need to bring the crafts and the fine arts together through architecture. With his friend Selwyn Image, Mackmurdo founded the Century Guild in 1882 to do just that. Influenced by Morris & Co., the Century Guild was an affiliation of independent architects, painters, and craftsmen who could provide architectural services as well as all the elements of an interior.

The Guild also produced a magazine, *The Hobby Horse*, which was yet another of Mackmurdo's influential undertakings. The magazine had a roster of

Adept with sinuous lines as well as straight ones, Mackmurdo designed his poppy side chair, 1883. The ebonized, mahogany fretwork of the back might appear to be high Art Nouveau, but it predates the style by a decade.

impressive contributors such as Ruskin and Oscar Wilde, and was also notable for its thoughtful visual presentation. Printed on handmade paper with custom-designed initials and ornaments, *The Hobby Horse* single-handedly elevated the craft of printing. On seeing a copy of the magazine, William Morris was said to have been inspired to start his own Kelmscott Press.

C. F. A. Voysey: Refined Simplicity

With a rectilinearity derived from Mackmurdo and an elegance reminiscent of the great Aesthetic movement designer E. A. Godwin, C. F. A. Voysey's furniture was slender and poised, employing simple, beautifully proportioned forms.

Despite its frankness, its straight lines, and its simplicity, Voysey's furniture was never clumsy or heavy. And although clearly influenced by country furniture, it pos-

Arts and Crafts designers from Voysey to Mackintosh responded to the furniture of the Aesthetic movement architect E. A. Godwin. Godwin's ebonized side chairs display the daring slenderness typical of his furniture. The asymmetrical patterns of their backs suggest his interest in the arts of the Orient.

IN DETAIL : THE FOOT AND THE FINIAL

ALTHOUGH not a prolific designer, A.H. Mackurdo did create furniture that made an impact. Most noted for its frequent use by other designers was the "Mackmurdo foot"— the bulbous swell at the bottom of a tapered leg. Stateside designers and manufacturers became especially fond of the element.

Another frequently copied Mackmurdo flourish was the broad, flat-topped finial. Both foot and finial are evident in Mackmurdo's desk on page 48. Round or square, the finial was favored by Voysey, Baillie Scott, and Liberty & Co. designers. (See Voysey's sideboard at top.)

Mackmurdo served as a bridge between the movement's founders and a younger generation of designers coming into their own in the 1890s. Although his designs were relatively few, they were thoroughly studied and often imitated.

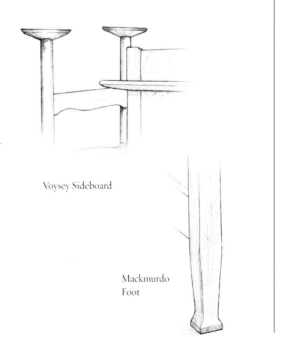

Voysey Sideboard

Mackmurdo Foot

sessed a refinement that kept it from appearing rustic. he typically built with unfinished solid oak and traditional joinery.

Voysey's program was uncomplicated: rectilinear elements fashioned as thinly as function would permit; wide overhanging horizontal planes playing off strong vertical ones; and carefully selected shallow curves to soften straight lines. His work was uncomplicated but skillfully executed.

Trained in London, Voysey drank deeply of the Arts and Crafts aesthetic. He was an early member of the Art Worker's Guild and contributed to the Arts and Crafts Exhibition Society shows from the start.

Voysey's Retail Contributions

Unlike such contemporaries as C. R. Ashbee and Ernest Gimson, however, Voysey did not share the movement's abhorrence of factory production or its inclination to make a craftsman of every designer. Indeed, throughout his career, Voysey supplemented his architectural commissions by selling designs to be manufactured and sold in stores.

Before he began attracting architectural clients, Voysey supported himself with commissions from manufacturers of textiles and wallpaper. His sprightly pattern designs, cleaner and less cluttered than popular Morris-inspired work,

---

IN DETAIL : VOYSEY'S VISUAL ANATOMY

LIKE HIS ARCHITECTURE, C. F. A. Voysey's furniture designs radiated simplicity and repose. Initially inspired by A.H. Mackmurdo's rectilinear furniture, Voysey quickly found his own voice. Featuring rudimentary forms, straight lines, and large, open areas of unvarnished wood, Voysey's furniture was essentially chaste. But he developed motifs and symbols that had personal meaning to him, such as the heart, bird, spade, and tree, and employed these decorative effects in moldings and hardware. Voysey introduced a slightly undulating line on stretchers, aprons, and moldings, which gave his otherwise rectilinear cabinets a distinctive grace.

Broad, flat-topped Mackmurdo finials became a signature element in Voysey's designs. In Voysey's work, the finials often capped slender posts, faceted and tapered.

The sparing use of a shallow double curve is characteristic on Voysey's cabinets.

Voysey's often-elaborate custom-designed hardware typically featured one of his symbolic motifs.

Voysey was concerned with the fitness of the materials being used. His furniture was built from only the best grades of wood— almost always white oak—so that it could be "left quite clean from the plane, without stain, varnish, or polish."

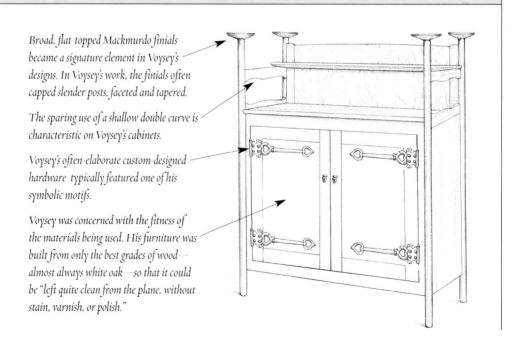

were an immediate success and showed Voysey to be the rare designer who was equally fluent working in two and three dimensions.

As an architect, Voysey specialized in building small houses. In a profession that traditionally awarded distinction based on designs for churches and public buildings, he became one of the first to attain international recognition based solely on residential work.

Voysey was as gifted in metal design as he was working in wood, stone, or fabric, and he styled most of the hardware and fittings for the houses he designed as well as for the furniture. Voysey's way with wood was always restrained, but he often used metal to give his furniture a decorative flourish.

The Artful Interior: M. H. Baillie Scott

Like Voysey, Mackay Hugh Baillie Scott was an architect who had no personal experience in the crafts but worked very closely and sympathetically with craftsmen. Also like Voysey, Baillie Scott specialized in building relatively modest country houses, or cottages, and turned his talented pen to the design of the light fixtures, built-ins, stained glass, fabrics, metalwork, hardware, and furniture that filled them.

Baillie Scott did not share the Arts and Crafts movement's qualms about machine production. Although he created decorative designs for specific houses, he also produced them for retailers. At one point he had a line of some 120 separate pieces of furniture in production.

Both Voysey and Baillie Scott considered the house a total work of art and were concerned that the furniture befit the structure. There is quite a leap, however, from Voysey's

A characteristic cottage from the drawing board of Baillie Scott shows his welcoming, vernacular style. The watercolor, which appeared in *The Studio* in 1904, is proof of his gifts as a painter as well as an architect. It exemplifies the Arts and Crafts preference for designing a garden along with the house.

Sheer sides and large unbroken volumes are typical of Baillie Scott case pieces. Built in 1903, this chest draws its energy from the contrast of a deep ebonized finish with the silver hardware and mother-of-pearl inlay.

No dark, brooding interiors for M. H. Baillie Scott. As this illustration from *The Studio* clearly shows, he was an advocate of strong colors in fabric and furniture.

Baillie Scott's exuberantly painted Manx piano demonstrates his preference for boxy forms with extensive surface decoration.

"Simplicity requires perfection in all its details, while elaboration is easy in comparison..."

C. F. A. Voysey, 1896

furniture to Baillie Scott's. For Baillie Scott, who had a background in painting, a piece of furniture was often a three-dimensional canvas. His pieces, especially his case goods, were often essentially sheer-sided boxes presenting themselves for adornment with paint, inlay, or custom hardware. Baillie Scott's eye for color and pattern provided many otherwise boxy cabinets with a considerable appeal.

The interiors of Baillie Scott's houses were vibrant with color. With their exposed ceiling timbers, leaded glass windows, cozy inglenooks, and extensive built-ins, they caught Stickley's eye and influenced the development of the American Arts and Crafts bungalow.

Liberty's and Heal & Son: Commercial Arts and Crafts in England

The Arts and Crafts movement wished to provide good design for the masses—without mass production. It was a paradox that affected every member of the movement. In England, most Arts and Crafts designers focused on creating good designs and avoiding factory production. But this meant they didn't produce affordable wares. Arthur Lasenby Liberty took a different approach. Liberty & Co., the department store he established in 1875, sold well-made and well-designed furnishings and fabrics at affordable prices.

But Liberty & Co.'s wares were made in factories. It was galling, too, to members of a movement that valued the efforts of the individual, that although the store employed many of the best designers of the era, Liberty's—as it was known—made no acknowledgement of them. Everything it sold was labeled simply "Liberty," in an effort to create name recognition among customers.

These choices made sound business sense, however. Liberty's thrived during the Arts and Crafts era, and after, delivering high quality English design to the international marketplace. Still famous today for its printed fabrics, the store also sold a wide and eclectic range of furnishings.

In the 1890s and 1900s, Liberty & Co. produced a line of furniture that combined Arts and Crafts and Art Nouveau influences in a blend reminiscent of the Glasgow style. Another line, designed by Leonard Wyburd, was stockier and more rustic, sharing much with Stickley's Craftsman line.

Heal & Son

Heal & Son, a London furniture retailer founded in 1810, also sold Arts and Crafts goods. Like Arthur Liberty, Ambrose Heal had a canny business sense and a big company to keep afloat. Unlike Liberty—and unlike most Arts and Crafts furniture designers—Heal had furniture-making experience. He had studied design and

Liberty's also carried furniture in a version of the Glasgow style. This mahogany secretary desk, designed for Liberty's in about 1903 by E. G. Punnett, is stylistically similar to designs offered by the Glasgow firm Wylie & Lochhead.

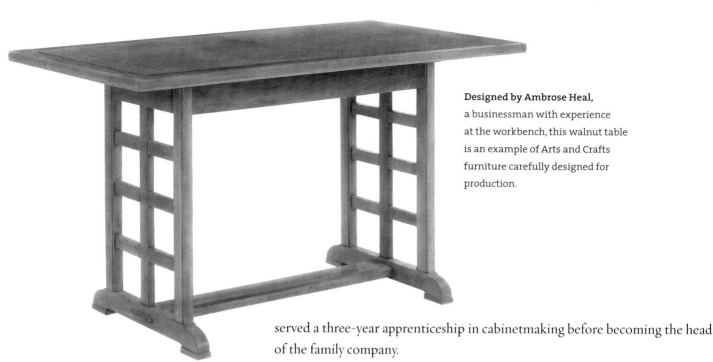

Designed by Ambrose Heal, a businessman with experience at the workbench, this walnut table is an example of Arts and Crafts furniture carefully designed for production.

served a three-year apprenticeship in cabinetmaking before becoming the head of the family company.

Like Liberty's, Heal & Son sold furniture in a range of styles in addition to Arts and Crafts. But Heal took a proprietary interest in his company's Arts and Crafts line, designing it all himself rather than hiring outside artists. The furniture was plain, undemonstrative, and very soundly built, possessing an appealing modesty and simplicity.

RELATED ARTS & CRAFTS

The Artistic House

Prior to the mid-19th century, house design was largely a concern of the upper class. During the second half of the 19th century, however, the industrial revolution created a burgeoning middle class. This new class had no need for baronial mansions but was attracted by the Ruskinian image of the rural cottage or modest home.

Such houses spawned a whole new concept in residential architecture. Interiors were laid out for function and simplicity. Fireplaces, stairways, and built-in furniture were given greater importance in terms of their decorative contribution to an interior. As architects became more involved in designing these interior elements, they also began to design the loose furnishings.

Design competitions for "Artistic" houses were sponsored by leading publications and organizations. Mackmurdo, Baillie Scott,

The entire interior was on the minds of most furniture makers in the Arts and Crafts era. Liberty & Co., which printed the scheme above for a drawing room in its catalog, offered a full interior-design service. The retailer produced fabrics, carpets, and lighting matched to its furniture.

Voysey, Mackintosh, and many other architects submitted experimental designs to such competitions. Not to be left out, most manufacturing and retailing concerns, such as Liberty & Co., Wylie & Lochhead, and Heal & Son, offered integrated design concepts to help their clients create their own artistic homes.

Liberty & Co. developed a brand of Arts and Crafts
furniture based on rural English forms and built
in solid oak. The decorative details that gave a piece
like this sideboard its Arts and Crafts flavor—curving
brackets and hammered hardware—were changed
from year to year to reflect the latest trends.

*"Utility . . . is in itself beauty
if rightly understood."*

Arthur Lasenby Liberty, 1900

England's Professional Caste

that spanned the fine and decorative arts during the Arts and Crafts era. Architects such as C. F. A. Voysey and M. H. Baillie Scott claimed the whole range of decorative media as their territory, designing houses and nearly everything within them. Both Voysey and Baillie Scott produced furniture that reflects a solid understanding of joinery and structure and a passion for fine craftsmanship. But unlike some other leading Arts and Crafts designers, neither man took a direct hand in making any of his furnishings.

Voysey and Baillie Scott both designed furniture for production as well as for custom commissions. And although the poor quality of mass-produced goods was one of the catalysts of the Arts and Crafts movement, many other leading designers followed suit. Liberty & Co. was one of the chief outlets for such professional designers. Heal & Son, a furniture retailer in London, also sold factory-produced furniture in the Arts and Crafts mode.

THE ARCHITECTURAL BASIS *of Voysey's furniture forms is evident in this game table and armchair from about 1904. The table's flat-topped finials were borrowed from A. H. Mackmurdo. The foursquare construction of both pieces is a delicate version of a building's firm stance.*

C. F. A. VOYSEY

C. F. A. Voysey's furniture married flat-sided cases with attenuated legs; straight lines and thin planes with carefully selected curves; unadorned solid-wood surfaces with gleaming decorative hardware. His work may have influenced Gustav Stickley's ponderous Craftsman furniture, but Voysey's pieces were always light and nimble. With their pared-down forms and rural flavor, Voysey's pieces had a modesty about them. His superb sense of proportion and his sensitive lines added refinement.

MUCH ABOUT VOYSEY'S *idiosyncratic approach to furniture design is exhibited in this oak writing desk of 1895. The delicately tapered octagonal posts and gently curved stretchers are only as strong and heavy as they need be. The vertical thrust of the piece is balanced by the broad, horizontal overhang of the top. Characteristically, Voysey's sole decorative flourish here is the custom hardware.*

C. F. A. VOYSEY COULD MAKE *substantial cabinets appear light on their feet. Rounded post legs, delicately double-curved side panels, and a twin top and shelf create the refined stance of this 1897 sideboard.*

M. H. BAILLIE SCOTT

Like his contemporary Voysey, M. H. Baillie Scott specialized in building small country houses and designing all of their furnishings. He drew on vernacular sources for his buildings as well as his furniture. Baillie Scott's furniture forms were often rudimentary variations of a cube. He made little use of moldings, carving, or shaping. Trained as a painter, he relied on color as much as form, often covering the flat surfaces of his furniture with intricate painted or inlaid designs.

THE PIANO WAS A STANDARD FEATURE *of the Victorian interior, which presented a problem for Arts and Crafts architects who liked to design everything in their houses. Baillie Scott responded by designing his own pianos. The plain form afforded space for his painterly embellishments.*

A SURPRISE AWAITED INSIDE *many Baillie Scott cabinets. Like Ashbee, he often designed pieces that were relatively plain on the outside but brightly painted or extensively inlaid on the inside. This ebonized secretary was conceived en suite for a 1903 exhibition in Dresden and built at the Deutsche Werkstatten.*

BAILLIE SCOTT'S *small mahogany cabinet from about 1901 was designed to be manufactured in quantity by John P. White's Pyghtle Works in Bedford, England. The Pyghtle Works had as many as 120 Baillie Scott designs in production. The cabinet's inlay is in holly, pewter, bone, and ebony.*

Liberty & Co.

Established in 1875, London's Liberty & Co. became by the turn of the century one of the world's most prominent retailers of furnishings. Founder Arthur Lasenby Liberty hired many of the era's leading designers, including the Scot George Walton and the German Richard Reimerschmid as well as Voysey and Baillie Scott. Liberty's sold furniture in a number of styles but became well known for a sophisticated blend of Arts and Crafts with Art Nouveau.

LIBERTY & CO.'S OWN *workshop produced much of the furniture the firm sold, but some pieces were subcontracted. This oak side chair by E. G. Punnett from 1901 was built by William Birch in the town of High Wycomb, the traditional center of chair manufacturing in England. Punnett's chair sold well for Liberty's for many years.*

THE LIBERTY & CO. LABEL *was the only identification on the firm's furniture, so the often prominent names behind the designs remained anonymous for decades. These side chairs show hints of Voysey, Walton, and Punnett, but their author's identity remains a mystery.*

LEONARD WYBURD LED *the Liberty & Co. furniture department during the Arts and Crafts era and contributed many designs for furniture and interiors to the company's catalog. A mahogany tea table inlaid with satinwood and harewood conveys Wyburd's functional approach to furniture design.*

HEAL & SON

Heal & Son had been selling furniture in London for nearly a century when the Arts and Crafts movement blossomed. The company produced pieces in a variety of styles, but Ambrose Heal admired the movement and designed his company's line of Arts and Crafts furniture himself. Trained as a cabinetmaker and a designer, Heal created pieces that are expressive of handwork yet economical to produce in large numbers.

BUILT IN CHESTNUT, *Heal & Son's dresser of 1903 is typical of the simplified cottage furniture for which the firm was noted. Using plain forms and little or no hardware, Heal's made furniture that was considerably less expensive than that sold at Liberty & Co. This dresser, closely based on one designed by Ford Madox Brown in the 1860s and sold by Morris & Co., expresses Ambrose Heal's affection for the simpler side of the Arts and Crafts style.*

HEAL & SON WAS RECOGNIZED *for its popular Arts and Crafts cottage furniture, but this walnut library table of 1929 shows the firm's ability to tackle more formal design with considerable success. The table's detailing recalls some of Gimson's Cotswolds furniture.*

Charles Rennie Mackintosh and the Glasgow Style

TODAY, A CENTURY AFTER being made, the furniture of Scottish designer Charles Rennie Mackintosh has achieved a level of acclaim that dwarfs most furniture made by his Arts and Crafts contemporaries. Yet at the turn of the twentieth century, he was not much noted in England. Mackintosh was weaned on Arts and Crafts ideas, but the furniture he created little resembled the work of his peers.

Beyond England, though, Mackintosh's furniture had a significant impact on designers. In Vienna, Mackintosh was celebrated by leaders of the Secessionist movement, which had strong ties to the Arts and Crafts aesthetic. In the United States, Charles Limbert applied a Mackintosh-derived scheme of plank construction and geometric cutouts to create production pieces that stand among the most visually distinctive American Arts and Crafts furniture. Another American, Harvey Ellis, drew deeply on Mackintosh's ornamental designs when he devised his much-admired line of inlaid furniture for Gustav Stickley.

In the 1890s, Glasgow's design scene was flourishing. Architects, artists, artisans, and designers, who were influenced variously by their Scottish heritage, Art Nouveau, Japanese design, and the Arts and Crafts movement, all contributed innovative art and ideas to what became known collectively as "the Glasgow Style." Mackintosh and a number of his contemporaries were also deeply influenced by the furniture of the Aesthetic movement of the 1870s and 1880s. Slender, elegant, and often ebonized, Aesthetic furniture had a lasting impact on Glasgow design.

Mackintosh: Style Innovator

"The craftsman of the future must be an artist."

C. R. Mackintosh, 1901

Charles Rennie Mackintosh produced Glasgow's most original and powerful furniture designs of the Arts and Crafts period, but his achievement was far from single-handed. The skillful interior designer George Walton preceded him in forging a style and approach that blended influences from the Arts and Crafts and Aesthetic movements. And the stable of furniture designers at the large firm Wylie & Lochhead made a strong contribution to the Glasgow Style as well. They were never innovators, but they became fluent in the style, applied it effectively across a wide range of pieces, and increased its popularity.

Along with Mackintosh, perhaps the designers most important to the genesis of Glasgow's signature style were three of his art-school friends: Herbert McNair and the sisters Frances and Margaret Macdonald. While still students in the early 1890s, the four friends collaborated on a variety of art projects from which emerged an original style. Full of sinuous lines, symbolism, and elongated, ghostly figures, the work attracted critical notice as well as many followers among craftsmen and designers. Before long, the group was referred to as "the Four." After 1895, Mackintosh's furniture took on the group's signature graphic style. Mackintosh later married Margaret Macdonald, with whom he collaborated on many interiors.

Mackintosh was as much an artist as an architect, and both are brought out in an 1893 portrait. When the photo was taken, Mackintosh was working for the architectural firm Honeyman and Keppie, while continuing his studies at the Glasgow School of Art.

The Power of Place

In the second half of the 19th century, Glasgow rose to a position of commercial influence second only to London in the British Empire. It was—as it remains—a distinctly Scottish city: hard-working, resourceful, independent, and international. All of these qualities were reflected in the vibrant strain of Arts and Crafts furniture that developed there in the 1890s and 1900s.

Gritty and bustling, brimming with craftsmen, Glasgow in the 1890s boasted vast shipyards and locomotive foundries. More than one-third of the world's total shipbuilding took place there. The ships and trains all needed furniture, so Glasgow rose to meet the demand. The supercharged economy supported companies such as Wylie & Lochhead, which employed as many as 1,700 craftsmen.

Glasgow was highly industrialized and its inhabitants were highly educated. To provide skilled craftsmen, designers, and managers for its many industries, the city spawned a string of impressive schools. Glasgow forged links to continental Europe through its position as a world supplier of ships and a port for international trade. For designers in Glasgow, the fashions of Paris and Vienna were as well known as those of London, and this worldliness was reflected in the city's furniture.

The Glasgow School of Art

Chief among the city's training schools was the Glasgow School of Art. Mackintosh attended the school in the 1880s and early 1890s, an experience which would prove to be pivotal for him in a number of ways.

The school's director, Francis Newbery, was a vigorous proponent of the Arts and Crafts movement. Newbery invited William Morris, C. F. A. Voysey, and other key designers to lecture and exhibit in Glasgow. He also expanded the role of crafts at the school. But most importantly, he simply encouraged creativity and individuality among his students.

For Mackintosh, Newbery's passionate advocacy would aid him in his early career. In 1896, Mackintosh won the commission to design a new building for the school. It was a plum job for so young an architect. Mackintosh met the challenge with a design that made innovative use of inexpensive materials. The school building helped establish his reputation and remains an architectural landmark.

Designed for production in 1895, an early Mackintosh dresser shows him combining curves with straight lines and creating strong shapes in the negative spaces. The awkwardness evident here would be gone a year or two later.

Mackintosh Emerges

Mackintosh designed more than 400 pieces of furniture in addition to a range of buildings before he turned to painting in his last years. Other architects who designed furniture for their buildings—Voysey, for instance—commonly

Mackintosh's wife, Margaret Macdonald, produced embroidered panels and repoussé metalwork to embellish Mackintosh's furniture. The carved motifs on the legs of this 1897 table from the Argyle Street Tea Room are evocative of Macdonald's Glasgow Style metalwork.

Like much of his furniture, Mackintosh's architecture had antecedents in the Scottish vernacular. Two perspective drawings of Mackintosh's Hill House from 1903, which appeared in *The Studio Yearbook*, reveal the way he brought a modernizing clarity to regional forms.

THE FOUR: MACKINTOSH, McNAIR, AND THE MACDONALDS

Charles Rennie Mackintosh was born in Glasgow in 1868, the fourth of 11 children. His father was a police superintendent. At 16, Mackintosh was apprenticed to a small architectural office and worked there while attending classes at the Glasgow School of Art until 1889. That same year, he joined the architectural firm of Honeyman and Keppie, where he became friends with Herbert McNair, who had joined the firm the previous year. Both men continued at the School of Art as evening students. In 1890, Mackintosh won a scholarship, and in 1891, spent three months traveling in Italy.

The sisters Frances and Margaret Macdonald studied at the Glasgow School of Art from 1890 to 1894. They became close friends and collaborators with Mackintosh and McNair. The beaten-lead panels, at right, were crafted by Margaret Macdonald for Mackintosh's 1903 smoker's cabinet. In 1894, "the Four," as they eventually became known, displayed together for the first time at the Institute of Fine Art's annual show. In 1899, Frances Macdonald and McNair were married, followed the next year by Mackintosh and Margaret.

specified the same furniture designs for a number of different commissions. But Mackintosh rarely repeated his.

Mackintosh's furniture developed through three phases. His earliest designs, made in the mid-1890s, had the most affinity with his English contemporaries Voysey and Baillie Scott. In the middle and longest period, the sinuous, decorative Glasgow Style was blended with—and in some cases yielded to—the hard-edged geometry and abstraction of Viennese Secession furniture. The third phase occurred after Mackintosh left Scotland for London in 1914. These last designs are a stark departure from the Glasgow Style and prefigure the arrival of Art Deco.

His designs show an awareness and appreciation for the principles that guided other Arts and Crafts designers. The artistic potential of everyday objects and the importance of function in the creation of forms were second nature to him. He expressed a decided affection for native architectural and furniture forms and the pursuit of the integrated interior.

When it suited his purpose, however, Mackintosh would compromise utility and the open expression of materials and joinery to experiment with pure form. Many of his chairs, for instance, traded comfort for visual impact, and he coated a number of pieces with opaque enamel—often white, sometimes black.

Unlike most Arts and Crafts designers, who relished the natural character of wood, Mackintosh frequently used opaque finishes for his furniture. By veiling both the wood grain and the structure of a piece, a painted finish enabled Mackintosh to emphasize overall form and decorative detailing.

Some of Mackintosh's furniture was not built to the highest levels of craftsmanship. This was not entirely his fault (although it evidently was not always his concern either). Whereas Voysey and Baillie Scott could have their designs executed in idealistic craft workshops such as Ashbee's Guild of Handicraft, Mackintosh had to content himself with local joinery shops that were oriented towards the bottom line. Glasgow's craftsmen were highly skilled but operated on tight production schedules and tended not to lavish time on fastidious handwork.

Mackintosh typically designed furniture to coordinate with his interiors. Almost all of his pieces were conceived for specific buildings—often to stand in specific spots. Yet his designs are strong enough to stand alone.

Tea Rooms

Kate Cranston was a godsend to Mackintosh. The owner of a number of upscale tea rooms in Glasgow, Cranston had a sharp business sense and an eye for daring design. The interiors Mackintosh created for her were the first where his abilities were not restrained by either a timid or underfunded client.

Most of Mackintosh's pieces were designed for specific interiors. Here, in his 1903-4 house for Kate Cranston, he created built-ins, light fixtures, and carpeting, as well as the furniture.

Designed by Mackintosh in 1903, the Salon de Luxe in the Willow Tea rooms has been faithfully restored. Today's visitors can experience a bygone era, right down to Mackintosh's menu.

The high-back chair for Cranston's Argyle Street Tea Room, with its tall, attenuated back, on page 62, was a complete departure from conventional chair forms. The back is more an assemblage of symbols than of chair parts. The cutout in the oval crest rail represents a bird or spirit, and the oval itself doubles as a halo over the head of anyone seated in the chair. When in use, these high-backed chairs literally separate the diners from the rest of the room, creating privacy. When empty, they appear like guardians or sentinels watching over a sacred space.

In his tea room commissions, Mackintosh found not only a superb client but the opportunity to create an extreme sort of interior. Tea rooms, which began to flourish in Glasgow in the 1880s, were fantasy spaces. People sought them out for more than simply the tea and scones. They offered escape from the demands of work and home, and from the soot and grime of the industrial city. Well designed, a tea room provided a vicarious experience of wealth or the bohemian life. It was transporting to eat, talk, and relax surrounded by silver furniture with mauve velvet seats and rose glass inserts.

Throughout his career, Mackintosh's best furniture was often dreamlike in its conjuring of exaggerated forms and symbolic imagery. In Kate Cranston's tea rooms, he controlled the design of every aspect of an interior, including light fixtures, wall coverings, stained glass, carpets, even menus and servers' uniforms.

The Glasgow Style's Other Contributors

In 1896 Mackintosh was hired to work with George Walton, the principal contractor on the Buchanan Street tea rooms of Miss Cranston. Walton, who had attended the Glasgow School of Art in the 1880s, had been in business for himself since 1888. Cranston helped propel his career with a tea room commission, which she would do for Mackintosh as well.

In the intervening years, Walton designed wall coverings, fixtures, and furniture. His strengths were in developing subtle color palettes and in designing the various aspects of a room in harmony. Early on he ordered furniture for his interiors, but by the mid-1890s, he began designing his own. His style was a long-limbed mixture of

Spirited and spiky, Walton's ebonized coat tree reveals his flair for reimagining historical forms.

George Walton's furniture often melded elements of Queen Anne— here, the cabriole legs—into compositions in keeping with the slender side of the English Arts and Crafts aesthetic.

"Art is the flower—life is the green leaf. Let every artist strive to make his flower a beautiful living thing."
C. R. Mackintosh, 1902

Arts and Crafts rectilinearity, curves and shapes derived from 18th-century furniture, and the litheness of Aesthetic movement furniture of designers such as E. A. Godwin.

Others designing in the Glasgow Style were E. A. Taylor, George Logan, and John Ednie, all members of the furniture firm of Wylie & Lochhead. This enormous firm furnished large ships, as well as supplied a great deal of Glasgow Style furniture, among other fashions, to the general public.

IN DETAIL : SKETCHING THE GLASGOW STYLE

E. A. Taylor's 1902 pen and color-wash design for a mantel and inglenook combines the subtle color palette and stencil patterns developed by George Walton with the attenuated heart, rose, and insect motifs of Mackintosh, McNair, and the Macdonald sisters. These elements were skillfully synthesized by the talented designers at Wylie & Lochhead to bring the Glasgow Style to its purest manifestation. This mantel and fireplace surround (bottom), were executed from the sketch. Once the structural elements were assembled, the decorative elements were simply applied as if on a two-dimensional work.

Mackintosh on the Wane

As World War I approached, Arts and Crafts careers were cut short. Mackintosh, despite having produced powerful work for two decades, saw his commissions dwindle.

Mackintosh had done almost all his designing in Scotland, but he had also earned a reputation abroad. His exhibit at the Vienna Secession's 1900 show had drawn praise and led to a friendship with Josef Hoffmann, one of the Secession's founders. Mackintosh's work had been published in magazines in England, on the Continent, and in the United States, and it was exhibited in Turin and even Moscow. Several prominent Arts and Crafts furniture designers in the United States had adopted elements of his style.

None of this exposure and appreciation helped much when things went sour. In 1914, with work scarce in Glasgow, Mackintosh and Macdonald moved to the coastal town of Walberswick. There is some evidence that they planned to move from there to Vienna, and that the outbreak of war scuttled any such plans. In 1916, they moved to London to start a practice. There was little work to be had in a city that had never embraced his style, so in 1923, after years of hardship, Mackintosh and Macdonald moved to the south of France. There they lived frugally off their savings while Mackintosh worked on watercolors. The paintings—many detailed studies of flowers—were notable, but failed to bring the prices Mackintosh hoped for. A planned book of his art never materialized. A year after returning to London, Mackintosh died of cancer in 1928, a forgotton figure. Margaret Macdonald lived until 1933.

The Glasgow firm Wylie & Lochhead employed a team of designers to produce furniture in a spectrum of styles. E. A. Taylor designed for them in the Glasgow mode, as evidenced in this cabinet with its Glaswegian hardware and leaded glass. The flared capitals evoke the furniture of Voysey.

Structure became the decoration in Mackintosh's ebonized oak chairs for the Willow Tea Room. These 1903 designs show a clear departure from the applied decoration of the Glasgow Style.

The Glasgow Style

GLASGOW'S STRONG CULTURAL TIES to London brought the ideas and aesthetic of the Arts and Crafts movement north in the 1880s and 1890s. But the Glasgow Style that crystallized in the mid-1890s blended European influences with English ones. Glasgow furniture partook of the simplifying thrust of English work but tended toward elongated forms and stylized, curvilinear decoration. Glaswegian designers shared the European enthusiasm for exploring old crafts, but the high-volume ethos of Glasgow's furniture manufacturers led to furniture made more quickly, often with less attention to craftsmanship.

C. R. Mackintosh is by far the best known of the Glasgow furniture designers, but excellent work was produced by others, notably George Walton, who ran his own interior-design company, and the firm of Wylie & Lochhead, which employed a roster of talented designers, some of whom specialized in a version of the Glasgow Style.

VERSATILITY WAS ONE *of George Walton's strengths. This armchair from about 1900, with patchwork of refined and country forms, is leagues removed from his elegant, historically based work.*

AN ELEGANT DOUBLE DROP-LEAF *table testifies to Walton's grounding in 18th-century English furniture and his affection for the English Arts and Crafts. The mahogany table was built in 1903 by J. S. Henry, a London firm.*

GEORGE WALTON STRUCK *an uncharacteristically modern note in his Holland cabinet of 1901. With its slender legs and thin overhanging top, the cabinet recalls C. F. A. Voysey's furniture, which Walton admired. But the curved and gridded doors give it a clean, distilled quality of its own.*

GEORGE WALTON

George Walton's furniture drew upon English Arts and Crafts sources as well as upon his background as a painter. An interior designer, he created furniture to be in harmony with a whole interior in the Arts and Crafts manner. More conservative and less original than Mackintosh's, Walton's furniture was more in keeping with his contemporaries in England. Still, it served as one of the foundation stones for the development of the Glasgow Style.

THE CONSERVATIVE END *of Walton's oeuvre includes these dining chairs from 1896. Oddly, the Sheraton form is rendered in round-sectioned stock that imitates bentwood furniture.*

WYLIE & LOCHHEAD

Wylie & Lochhead was a commercial concern, huge even by Glasgow standards. It was involved in fitting out ships as well as furnishing offices and houses. Its retail showroom helped make the Glasgow Style a household name. Credit for most of the firm's Glasgow Style furniture is attributed to staff designers E. A. Taylor, John Ednie, and George Logan.

A STRAIGHTFORWARD SIDEBOARD *in the English Arts and Crafts mode, this piece from 1901 by E. A. Taylor defines one end of Wylie & Lochhead's design range. In its straight lines and hammered copper hardware, the piece is quite similar to work just then emerging from Gustav Stickley's Craftsman workshops.*

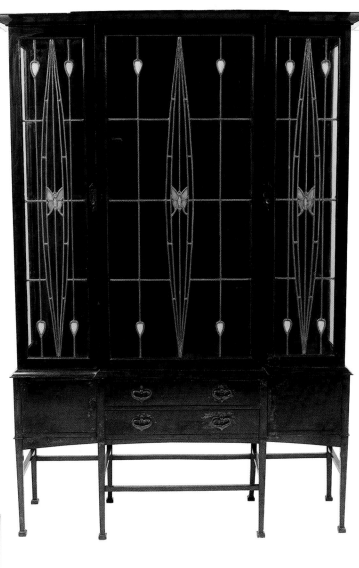

SLENDER LEGS, A KNIFE-THIN crown molding, and elaborate leaded glasswork place Taylor's 1901 display cabinet within the Glasgow Style. Taylor designed the piece for the international exhibition held in Glasgow in 1901.

THE INLAID DESIGN on Taylor's mahogany dresser implies a connection with English Arts and Crafts furniture, where rose motifs often appeared. The peak on the top of the mirror and the pierced hearts on the apron were signature Glasgow touches.

E. A. TAYLOR STRUCK *a far different mood in his ebonized hutch, which echoes Mackintosh in its opaque finish and employs Glasgow Style motifs in its panel decorations and its silver hardware. The peculiar peak above the open shelving is another mark of the Glasgow Style.*

© Ernest A. Taylor, The Montreal Museum of Fine Arts,
Photo: Montreal Museum of Fine Arts, Chrisitne Guest

WYLIE & LOCHHEAD REACHED *its upper register with this walnut folding screen designed by George Logan in 1901. Likely an exhibition piece, it employs extensive inlays in silver, mother-of-pearl, turquoise, and red amethyst. The center panel is a pen-and-ink drawing by Logan's wife, the noted Glasgow Style illustrator Jessie King.*

GEORGE LOGAN'S HEXAGONAL TABLE *was produced for the 1901 Glasgow exhibition. Like many other Wylie & Lochhead pieces, it is a blend of contemporary and historical elements. Its attenuated, faceted legs and arched skirts are reminiscent of Walton's style.*

AN EVOCATIVE DESIGN *in blue glass and zinc on the backsplash and an exuberant apron turn a standard Victorian table into an interesting Glasgow Style washstand. John Ednie designed the hybrid piece for Wylie & Lochhead.*

CHARLES RENNIE MACKINTOSH

Charles Rennie Mackintosh played a central part in developing the Glasgow Style. But unlike the commercial concern of Wylie & Lochhead, he quickly left it behind to explore new forms. By the early 1900s, as he came in contact with the like-minded designers of the Vienna Secession, geometry replaced sinuous ornament in many of his pieces. Although Mackintosh's pieces are powerful when seen in isolation, most were designed to fit with other pieces and furnishings in specific interiors.

THE POWER OF STARK SQUARES *is melded with organic ornament in Charles Rennie Mackintosh's 1904 desk for Hill House. It is built of ebonized oak and features mother-of-pearl inlay.*

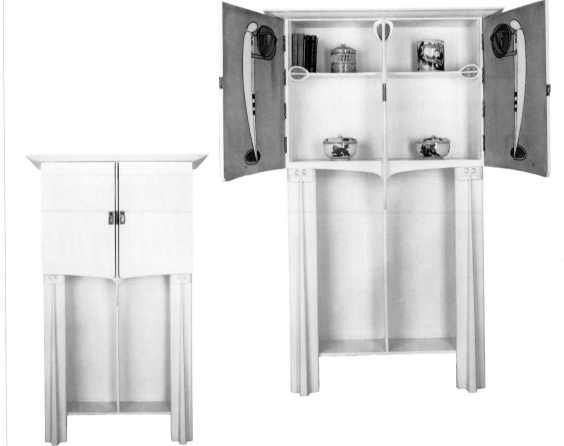

ALMOST DEVOID OF DECO-RATION *when closed, this cabinet opens to reveal images of a personal symbolism evidently connected to Rosicrucian philosophy. A pair of these cabinets was commissioned in 1902, and Mackintosh had a nearly identical pair made for his own use in his Mains Street flat. Mackintosh used an enamel finish to gain complete control of the form, then turned his attention to manipulating the decorative details.*

MACKINTOSH BEGAN DESIGNING *tall-backed chairs in the late 1890s. These chairs, designed for the Ingram Street Tea Room, include one of Mackintosh's earliest uses of decorative square cutouts. The tall and medium-height chairs were made in 1900; the low version was created in 1912 by cutting down the backs of taller chairs.*

DISTILLED GEOMETRY *was both structure and statement in Charles Rennie Mackintosh's 1904 chair for the Willow Tea Room. Designed to serve as both a seat and a screen, it's one of Mackintosh's most powerful visual statements. The gridded back incorporates an abstract image of a willow tree.*

EPITOMIZING MACKINTOSH'S WORK *in the Glasgow Style, this 1899 smoker's cabinet features copper repoussé panels by his wife, Margaret Macdonald. The carvings closely relate to the graphic design produced by the Four.*

As successfully as any architect *of the Arts and Crafts era, Mackintosh realized Morris's vision of the integrated interior. Mackintosh's method is illustrated here in the upstairs studio of his Mains Street flat as re-created in Glasgow's Hunterian Art Gallery. He designed each piece to stand in specific rooms and coordinated colors and embellishments of the furniture with carpet, drapes, wall tiles, and lighting.*

Continental Europe

The IDEAS OF THE English Arts and Crafts movement found many passionate supporters in continental Europe. Among designers in Scandinavia and especially in Germany and Austria, the writings of Ruskin and Morris and the activities of such designers as C. R. Ashbee, C. F. A. Voysey, and C. R. Mackintosh had a profound impact.

The visual connections were not always obvious. Much of the most powerful Arts and Crafts-influenced continental furniture, such as Austrian designer Josef Hoffmann's table, was strikingly different in form, detail, and finish from anything being made in London at the time. In Germany and Austria, as it did elsewhere, the Arts and Crafts philosophy produced work in a broad stylistic range.

Hoffmann's furniture, with abstract geometric patterning, concealed joinery, and often opaque finishes, looked more like an anticipation of Modernism than a reflection of English Arts and Crafts. Yet the work was fostered in an environment consciously modeled on the English example.

Much of Hoffmann's work, for instance, was made at his *Wiener Werkstatte,* or Viennese Workshop, a large cooperative that produced a range of high-quality crafts. The *Wiener Werkstatte* was directly inspired by Ashbee's Guild and School of Handicraft, which Hoffmann had visited in England. During the same period, many other Arts and Crafts-style workshops were founded in Germany.

On the whole, Continental designers dispalyed a far more open attitude toward mass production than those in England.

The Arts and Crafts concept of unity in the arts—the breaking down of the barrier between the fine and decorative arts—was strongly embraced on the continent, as was the idea of the house as an encompassing work of art. The various German and Austrian workshops produced everything from cutlery to coat hooks, in addition to furniture.

Arts and Crafts in Austria

"Carve stoops and stoves, make doors and cupboards, storm the china factories. . . . Yes, painter, build the houses yourself."

Carl Larsson, 1889

In May 1897, a group of progressive artists, architects, and designers withdrew from Vienna's primary art club, the Kunstlerhaus. Seeking less-restricted roles for artists and designers, they formed their own exhibition society, which they called "the Vienna Secession." The group decried the widespread adoption of historical styles and the flood of poorly designed goods on the market. It also sought to unify the crafts and fine arts and to encourage the development of a new style to fit the moment.

The Vienna Secession bore striking parallels to the Arts and Crafts Exhibition Society of nearly a decade earlier. The Secessionists, as they were known, consciously reached out to their contemporaries in England. But with such talented members as the painters Gustav Klimt and Koloman Moser, and architects Otto Wagner and Josef Hoffmann, the Vienna Secession had the power to command international attention in its own right.

IN DETAIL : HOFFMANN'S MAGIC MACHINES

JOSEF HOFFMANN had no aversion to using machines to do what they did best, which was to make identical parts with great precision. Like his English counterparts, he was opposed to using machines to mimic handwork. But for Hoffmann, machine technology opened up new design possibilities. His abstract version of the Morris chair, the *Sitzmachine,* an example of how, in Hoffmann's furniture, standardized, machine-produced parts doubled as decorative elements. Hoffmann's willingness to explore the machine's potential helped in creating a light, delicate style that was in marked contrast to the furniture by Ashbee and Baillie Scott which had so inspired Hoffmann just a few years earlier.

Hoffmann drew from abstract geometry for his signature ornamentation. Precise cutouts were created by machine using templates.

Hoffman used standardized steam-bent frames for the chair's structure. Steam-bending provides strength and an elegant linear form and is ideal for mass production.

Where the chair required screw-blocks, Hoffmann extended the geometric theme with perfect spheres at the joints.

An opaque finish was a rarity in Arts and Crafts furniture, but Hoffmann chose to paint or lacquer most of his furniture, hiding the materials and emphasizing the structure.

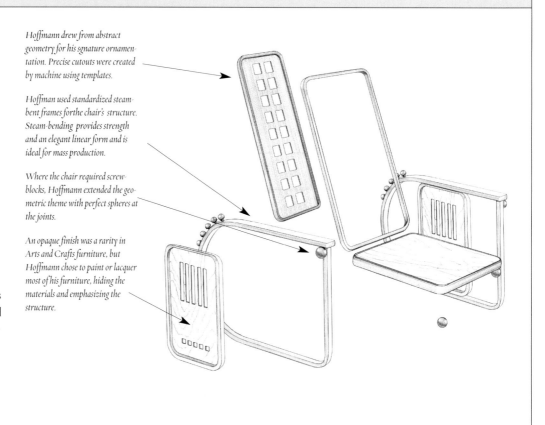

Mackintosh on the Mainland

The Vienna Secession mounted a series of successful exhibitions. In 1900, for their eighth show, they invited Mackintosh to contribute. His exhibit caused something of a sensation. One critic found the Mackintosh room ghastly and unlivable; another said it ranked among the best works of art in recent memory. His work was generally embraced by members of the Vienna Secession, and was particularly praised by Hoffmann, with whom he became friends.

Hoffmann's furniture has frequently been compared with that of Mackintosh. There are tantalizing similarities. Both Mackintosh and Hoffmann had roots in Art Nouveau as well as in the Arts and Crafts movement, and their furniture balanced curves with rectilinear elements. Both men were inclined towards geometric ornament and abstraction in their designs. And both resisted the Arts and Crafts conventions of exposed joinery and natural finishes, preferring instead to heighten the graphic power of their pieces by coating them with opaque paints and lacquers, often in black or white.

One distinction between them is that Hoffmann's furniture, with none of the tendrils and symbolism of Mackintosh's, tended far more toward geometric purity. Some critics claim that Mackintosh's work changed Hoffmann's; others say the reverse is true. Either way, it's clear both of these brilliant designers benefited from their transcontinental friendship.

Vienna's Great Guild:
Wiener Werkstatte

When Hoffmann and Moser founded the *Wiener Werkstatte* in 1903, they wrote that they hoped to create a workplace which, "amid the joyful hum of arts and crafts, would be welcome to anyone who professes faith in Ruskin and Morris."

The *Werkstatte,* which produced a spectrum of high-quality custom-designed furnishings, employed as many as 100 craftsmen and bustled along for three

Austrian designer Wilhelm Schmidt's armchair of 1902 illustrates his affinity with Mackintosh, who built a number of chairs with a similar cubic format.

© 2002 Historical Design, Inc., New York

A Viennese version of the Morris chair, Hoffmann's *Sitzmachine* uses structural elements for decorative effect.

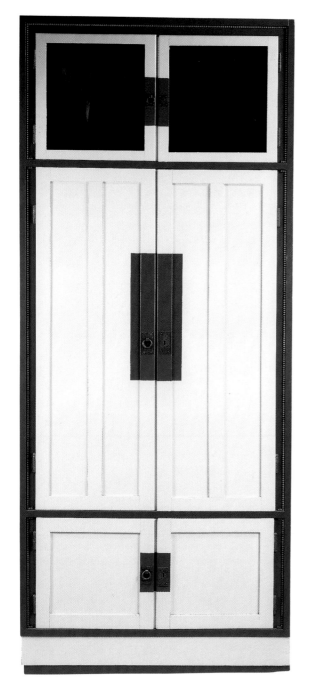

Koloman Moser who began his career as a painter, shows off his gift for flat composition in this cabinet.

© The Metropolitan Museum of Art, Gift of Cynthia Hazen Polsky, 1988.
Photo © 1989 The Metropolitan Museum of Art

decades. It proved to be among the most successful guilds of the Arts and Crafts era.

Both Hoffmann and Moser strove to improve the quality of the everyday object. They were devout advocates of *gesamtkunstwerk*— the idea that the house was a total, integrated environment in which the designs for the architectural shell, the furniture, metalwork, carpets, light fixtures, and even linens, china, and flatware were all to flow from the same designer's pen. In this, and in their unwavering commitment to the highest standards of craftsmanship, the designers of the *Wiener Werkstatte* were clearly philosophical brethren of the English Arts and Crafts practitioners.

The *Wiener Werkstatte* did not emulate Ashbee's ambitious program for social reform, but it did create an environment in which designers worked closely with makers. The maker's initials appeared alongside those of the designer on each piece the *Werkstatte* produced. And craftsmen were awarded royalties just like the designers.

Hoffmann, in common with his Austrian and German colleagues, exhibited none of the English Arts and Crafts movement's squeamishness toward machinery and industry, even though he was critical of typical mass-produced goods. The *Wiener Werkstatte's* impeccably crafted furnishings required extensive handwork, but there was no hesitation to use machines or make objects in batches if quality could be maintained.

Some of Hoffmann's most famous designs, in fact, were made in very large-scale production by the firm of J. & J. Kohn. Kohn, whose factories turned out thousands of pieces of bentwood furniture each day, gave Hoffmann's powerfully graphic pieces international exposure from 1901 to 1914.

A willingness to tailor designs for machine production set Hoffmann apart from most of his English Arts and Crafts contemporaries. Hoffmann created this chair for Thonet, the bentwood furniture manufacturer.

Ruskin and Morris in Deutschland

Arts and Crafts workshops popped up all across Germany in the late 1890s and early 1900s. Inspired by Ruskin, Ashbee, and other English pioneers, these shops shared many Arts and Crafts ideals, prizing craftsmanship, honest construction, and a simplified, regional style. But a lack of interest in social reform and a penchant for machine production distinguished the German shops from their English antecedents. It was the embrace of the machine and industry that put the stamp on German furniture of the era, which led toward the Bauhaus, Modernism, and, eventually, the repudiation of the pastoral Arts and Crafts.

The two most prominent German workshops were the *Werkstatten* in Munich, headed by the gifted designer Richard Riemerschmid, and in Dresden, led by Riemerschmid's brother-in-law, the designer Karl Schmidt. Like most of their contemporaries in Germany, Riemerschmid and Schmidt produced furniture in the late 1890s in the style known as *Jugendstil*—a blend of Arts and Crafts, Art Nouveau, and local forms.

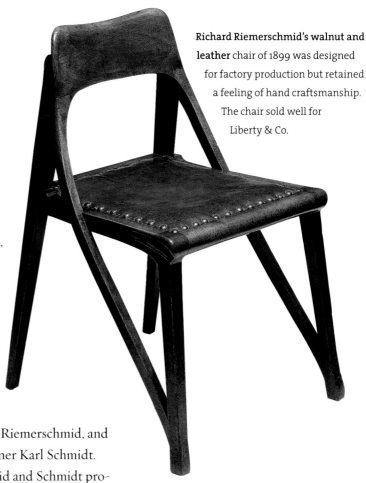

Richard Riemerschmid's walnut and leather chair of 1899 was designed for factory production but retained a feeling of hand craftsmanship. The chair sold well for Liberty & Co.

RELATED ARTS & CRAFTS

Art Nouveau: The Sinuous Counterpart

Art Nouveau took its name from Maison de l'art Nouveau, the Paris shop opened in 1895 by influential importer and retailer Siegfried Bing. With its extravagant curlicues and concealed, sometimes questionable construction, Art Nouveau was everything that Arts and Crafts wasn't.

Among Arts and Crafts practitioners in England, Art Nouveau was often derided. But in France, Italy, and Belgium, it was the rage. In Austria and Germany, a blend of Art Nouveau with English Arts and Crafts influences created a local style called *Jugendstil*. Art Nouveau also made an impact in Scotland, where Mackintosh and George Walton incorporated some of the style's sinuous curves into their work.

In France, where Art Nouveau reached its peak, the style grew from the country's ornamental historic furniture forms, which were often highly sculptural and gave no hint as to the underlying construction. Jugendstil designs used similar flowing curves but confined them to cutouts, surface decoration, and edge shaping, which left the underlying construction easily discernable, as shown in the cabinet (at right) by Belgian designer Gustave Serrwrier-Bovy. This form of Art Nouveau appeared in many furniture designs at British retailers Liberty's and Wylie & Lochhead, as well as in those of American designers Charles Limbert and Charles Rohlfs.

© The Metropolitan Museum of Art, Gift of Mr. and Mrs. Lloyd Macklowe, 1981. Photo © 1982 The Metropolitan Museum of Art

By the early 20th century, however, these designers were moving away from the flowing lines and structural curiosities of Art Nouveau toward a straighter, sturdier style consciously suited to machine production. In 1904, Riemerschmid designed a line of furniture called, explicitly, *machinmobel,* or factory-made furniture, for which interchangeable parts were produced in large numbers. Riemerschmid had taken a decisive step away from one of the founding principles of the Arts and Crafts movement, but he was a nimble enough designer that his furniture possessed something of a handmade feel despite being produced by machine.

A Push toward Standardization

A second move in the same direction came in 1907 with the founding of the *Deutscher Werkbund.* The *Werkbund,* or workers guild, was a trade organization established by architects and designers that was intended to raise the level and profitability of German design. The idea was to bring designers and craftsmen together with captains of industry. The *Werkbund* also hoped to promote standardized

"It is absolutely no longer possible to convert the masses. . . . It is all the more our duty to make happy those few who turn to us."

Josef Hoffmann, 1903

With a distilled form and no surface decoration, Henri van de Velde's salon table from 1898 seems to prefigure the machine aesthetic of the Bauhaus. But the Belgian van de Velde was opposed to mass production and focused instead on providing impeccably crafted furnishings for the wealthy.

© 2002 Historical Design, Inc., New York

designs—such as Riemerschmid's *machinmobel*—which would increase profitability and establish a recognizably German style.

Many of the best German and Austrian designers of the time—from Riemerschmid, Bruno Paul, and Peter Behrens to Josef Olbrich and Hoffmann—joined forces and designed for the *Werkbund.*

This drive to integrate art and industry prompted a countermovement within Germany among designers such as the Belgian-born architect and educator Henri van de Velde, who valued above all the individuality of the designer.

Ernst Ludwig's Legacy

The Arts and Crafts movement traveled to Germany and Austria in Ruskin's books, Morris's writings, and in the pages of *The Studio* magazine. *The Studio,* founded in London in 1893, quickly developed an international reach as it covered architecture, painting, sculpture, and the decorative arts in a nonhierarchical mixture. *The Studio* covered Art Nouveau but was particularly strong in championing the designers of the Arts and Crafts movement. German designers saw work by Voysey, Baillie Scott, and Ashbee in *The Studio,* and many were inspired to visit England to see these men and their work firsthand.

One German—Ernst Ludwig, the Grand Duke of Hesse—was so deeply impressed by what he saw in *The Studio* that he invited Baillie Scott and Ashbee to design interiors for his palace at Darmstadt. These rooms, well-covered in the media, captured the imagination of German designers.

The Grand Duke went on to establish an art colony at Darmstadt in 1899. He invited German and Austrian painters, designers, and architects to design houses and furnishings. The colony was an attempt to bring craftsmen and designers into close contact in hopes of producing a tradition of crafts of superior quality. The Darmstadt colony was a Ruskin-inspired utopia, and like similar communities attempted in the United States and England, it was relatively short-lived, closing down within a decade.

At the time, it was said that the two tendencies in German decorative arts—toward craftsmanship and toward industry—were examples of "the utopia of the pulse" and the "utopia of the piston." With the rise of the machine aesthetic of the Bauhaus and the Modern movement, the piston was proven—at least temporarily—more powerful.

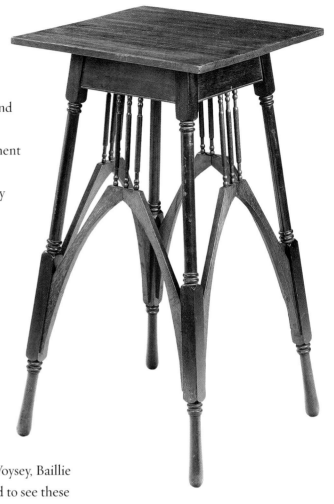

German Grand Duke Ernst Ludwig brought English interiors and furniture to the continent. Ludwig, discovered Baillie Scott, Voysey, and Ashbee through *The Studio* magazine and commissioned furnishings from them. Baillie Scott's 1898 table was produced by the Guild of Handicraft.

The Vienna Secession

WHETHER PRODUCING FURNITURE, ceramics, or metalwork, the designers of the Vienna Secession exhibited high standards of craftsmanship and stressed the interdependence of form and function. After an early period that reflected the influence of Art Nouveau and the English Arts and Crafts, designers such as Josef Hoffmann and Koloman Moser forged a new style notable for sharp-edged geometric forms. In its repetitive cutouts and elemental structure, their furniture had a machine-made feeling, but it was often handmade in exquisite materials. The design reforms worked out by the members of the Vienna Secession—as well as in the various *Werkstatten* in Austria and Germany—were influential in the founding of the Bauhaus school in 1919 and the launch of Modernist design.

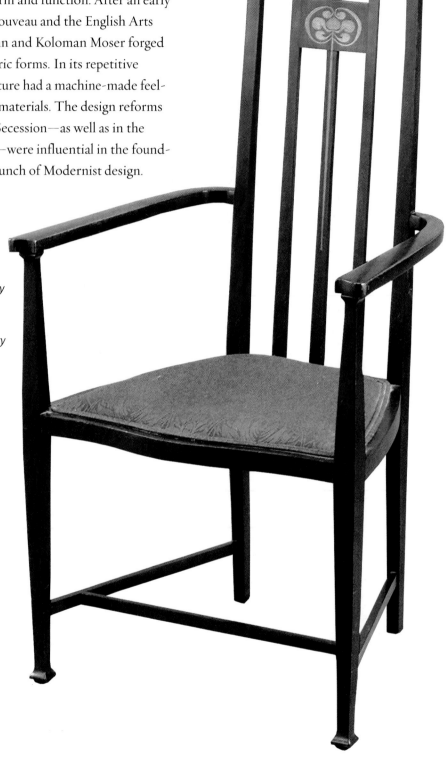

SLENDER AND SIMPLE *with shallow curves in a rectilinear frame, this mahogany armchair by Joseph Maria Olbrich from around 1900 shows a strong similarity to work by Englishmen Baillie Scott and Voysey as well as to Scotsman George Walton.*

JOSEPH MARIA OLBRICH

One of the founders of the Vienna Secession, Joseph Olbrich was the architect of the Secession's famous exhibition building. Like many of his colleagues in the Secession and in the Arts and Crafts movement in general, Olbrich had a hand in a wide range of projects, designing posters, wallpapers, lighting, cutlery, embroidery, and illustrations as well as furniture and buildings. His furniture combined English Arts and Crafts and Art Nouveau influences with classical ones.

THE INFLUENCE OF ENGLISH *Arts and Crafts was evident in the early years of the Vienna Secession. With its wafer-thin top and narrow, tapered posts, Josef Hoffmann's 1902 cabinet is indebted to Voysey. The cabinet's stained oak exterior opens to a blond interior of bird's-eye maple. Both the bright interior and the cabinet's overall blocky form are reminiscent of C. R. Ashbee.*

© 2002 Historical Design, Inc., New York

JOSEF HOFFMANN

The most powerful designs of the continental branch of Arts and Crafts came from the pen of Josef Hoffmann, a key figure in the Vienna Secession. The style he developed at his *Wiener Werkstatte* had the honesty and impeccable craftsmanship championed by the Arts and Crafts movement but utilized boldly abstract and graphic forms that still look modern a century later.

FORM AND FUNCTION *go hand in glove in this vitrine in ebonized beech designed by Hoffmann and mass-produced by J. & J. Kohn. The economical structure, composed of three bentwood frames, is made rigid by the side and back panels. The small spheres Hoffmann used to reinforce critical joints are an open expression of machine production and a witty parallel to the exposed hand joinery found in so much English Arts and Crafts furniture.*

© 2002 Historical Design, Inc., New York

JOSEF HOFFMANN'S 1905 CHAIR *in beech, sycamore veneer, ebony inlay, and leather demonstrates the flexibility of his machine-based design system. Although appearing quite substantial, it is made with only a few standardized parts: two bentwood frames, two veneer ovals, four posts, and an upholstered seat and back.*

© 2002 Historical Design, Inc., New York

KOLOMAN MOSER

A painter by training, Koloman Moser designed furniture that reflected his background in two-dimensional art. One trend in his furniture was toward plain surfaces painted white with black trim to create strong abstract compositions. Another, also utilizing flat surfaces, was toward allover inlaid decoration with themes from classical antiquity. Moser was instrumental in the founding of the Vienna Secession and was Hoffmann's partner in the *Wiener Werkstatte.* Moser left the *Werkstatte* in 1907 and returned to painting.

MOSER'S 1903 FALL-FRONT DESK
has links to the severe geometric forms and rich surface decoration of Baillie Scott's furniture. Moser's piece is also reminiscent of the blocky, entirely veneered cabinets of the mid-19th-century Biedermeier style. The desk was made of thuya, satinwood, and brass, and utilizes ancient Greek motifs, a favorite of the Secessionists.

Gustav Stickley and His Brothers

Gustav Stickley's stark, straight-lined furniture established the style that scores of other manufacturers would emulate to create the Mission boom in the first decade of the 20th century. This 1903 secretary, designed by Harvey Ellis for Stickley, retains the boldness of the first Craftsman designs while showcasing Ellis's flair for proportion and composition.

FAR MORE PROMINENTLY than any other designer, Gustav Stickley has come to represent American Arts and Crafts furniture. It is not only in hindsight that Stickley looms large: He had a profound influence on his contemporaries. His Craftsman Workshops did not build the most Mission furniture—there were many factories that outstripped his in total production. And Craftsman designs, although strong, were not necessarily the most refined or most original of the American Arts and Crafts movement.

But the visual impact of his furniture was powerful. Stark, straight-lined, and stripped of decoration, his Craftsman designs possessed a daring purity. And the coherent way that Stickley applied the style across a range of pieces gave his furniture an even stronger presence. Customers were immediately attracted to the furniture, and so were other manufacturers, who saw in its simplicity a style perfectly suited to machine production. Among those who followed in Stickley's footsteps were four of his brothers, whose companies all made Mission furniture.

Gustave Stickley himself was a large-scale manufacturer with as many as 200 employees, and the size of his operation helped establish his reputation. He was also the publisher of *The Craftsman,* which was the leading American journal of the Arts and Crafts movement. The magazine served Stickley both as a platform and as something of a pedestal.

Stickley combined the ideals and some of the crusading spirit of a social reformer with the manufacturing and marketing savvy of an experienced furniture producer. He believed in the power of furnishings to create a simpler, more rooted, more fulfilling life. But he also believed in the need to make a profit. It was a combination that proved exceptionally potent.

Origins of the Style

"I did not realize at the time that in making those few pieces of strong, simple furniture, I had started a new movement. Others saw it and prophesied a far-reaching development. To me it was only furniture; to them it was religion. And eventually it became religion with me as well."

Gustav Stickley, c. 1911–14

The furniture we recognize today as Stickley's is but one of many styles he explored in his long career. When Stickley brought out his first Arts and Crafts furniture in 1900, he was 42 years old and had been involved in furniture manufacturing since his early teens. Like most American furniture manufacturers at the time, Stickley made furniture in a range of derivative historical styles—Victorian, Queen Anne, Windsor, Colonial, Shaker—and he knew how to do so efficiently and in large quantities. His new furniture, however, was different because it came with some conviction.

Throughout the 1890s, Americans had learned about Arts and Crafts designs and ideals from magazines, books, and international expositions. Arts and Crafts societies were established in several cities, and many small craft shops and cooperatives founded on Arts and Crafts principles began producing well-designed, high-end work in metal, ceramics, textiles, glass, and furniture.

Stickley had read John Ruskin and William Morris, whose books and lectures on aesthetics launched the Arts and Crafts movement.

The plainness of Stickley's Craftsman furniture is the more remarkable when seen in comparison to other furniture available at the time. These anonymous late-Victorian chairs are suggestive of the hodgepodge of historical revivalism and classical misinterpretation that prevailed in the 1890s.

English furniture proved a key inspiration for Gustave Stickley's Craftsman line. The trip filled him with Arts and Crafts idealism and design ideas. This table, which Stickley produced in 1901, is a nearly direct copy of a piece by the English designer M. H. Baillie Scott.

GUSTAV STICKLEY
(1858–1942)

Born March 9, 1858, in Osceola, Wisconsin, Gustav was the oldest of 11 children. His father, Leopold, worked as a stonemason. Gustav became his apprentice at an early age. It was an experience he always resented. When Gustav was 12 his mother took the children to Pennsylvania. There, the Stickley boys found employment in their uncle's factory—The Brandt Chair Company. Later, Gustav and four of his brothers opened their own furniture retail and wholesale store in nearby Binghamton, New York.

In 1893, Gustav and Elgin A. Simons founded the Stickley & Simons Company, which made furniture in an array of historical styles. Stickley bought out Simons in 1899 to form the Gustav Stickley Company. Within two years he launched the famous Craftsman line. Craftsman furniture was a rousing success, and spawned a magazine, a business in bungalow plans, and much else. In 1913, Stickley moved his retail and publishing operations to Manhattan. But the costly move was ill-timed. The popularity of the furniture was plummeting, and Stickley's empire collapsed. He declared bankruptcy in 1915 at age 57 and entered a long, twilit retirement.

Their ideas for social reform and honest craftsmanship appealed to Stickley but did not much influence his work until 1898, when he traveled to England and was exposed to English Arts and Crafts: Ruskin's and Morris's ideas in action.

Stickley absorbed how some English Arts and Crafts designers, inspired by objects of preindustrial craftsmanship, utilized rectilinear forms and forthright construction. A refectory table by M. H. Baillie Scott, for example, clearly served as the basis for Stickley's own table above.

American Influences

Although Stickley's trip to England was a watershed, he had long been favorably impressed by the straightforward simplicity of Shaker designs, and some Craftsman furniture is clearly indebted to the architectural flavor of Frank Lloyd Wright's furniture. For a few years, Stickley produced a line of spindle furniture to capitalize on the popularity of Prairie School architecture in the Midwest.

Stickley's Cutting Edge

Stickley's furniture was designed to be manufactured competitively. The use of machines and techniques of mass production might appear antithetical to the founding principles of the Arts and Crafts movement. But he didn't see it that way.

Unlike many of the well-to-do theorists and designers of the movement, Stickley was pressed into manual labor—stonework—before he had reached his teens. He never felt the romance of hard labor. He insisted upon good craftsmanship but thought that if a job could be accomplished by machine, so much the better. Still, the popular appeal of the movement's strong message about the sanctity of handwork was not lost on him, and he made use of it in promoting his furniture.

As part of Gustav Stickley's pioneering New Furniture line introduced in 1900, this innocent-looking plant stand helped start the trend toward simplified, straight-lined furniture. Stickley's New Furniture was a hit at the Grand Rapids exposition where it debuted, and other manufacturers quickly followed Stickley's lead.

"The hope of reform would seem to be in the direction of a return to the spirit which animated the workers of a more primitive age, and not merely to an imitation of their method of working."

Gustav Stickley, 1906

Essence of the Craftsman Style

The Craftsman style was, in some ways, an antistyle. It was the stripping away of ornament and the banishment of embellishment. At a time when the furniture industry was dominated by historic revivalism and period reproduction work, Craftsman furniture searched for what was elemental in a piece of furniture and discarded everything else. It was furniture reduced to structure.

But if Craftsman furniture was devoid of decoration, it was full of meaning: These were not simply designs for furniture but blueprints for a way of life. The straight lines, flat planes, and exposed joinery of a Craftsman piece spoke of forthrightness and honesty. Its plainness was a mark of simplicity and humility. Its heaviness implied stability and rootedness.

All these elements and ideas are traceable to English Arts and Crafts designers, but in Stickley's hands, where they were reworked with a view toward production and profit, they were distilled into a line of furniture of remarkable consistency and clarity.

Stickley's manufacturing know-how enabled him to follow the Arts and Crafts design precepts of good craftsmanship and honest construction without getting mired in expensive handwork. His extensive use of through mortise-and-tenon joints, for instance, conveyed an impression of strength and solidness and considerable craftsmanship. But by standardizing parts and joint sizes, Stickley was able to cut most of the joinery by machine.

Design Evolution

Stickley's Craftsman line did not remain static. It evolved in response to pressure from the many other manufacturers of Mission furniture and also in response to the sensibilities of the various designers Stickley employed. His best designers included La Mont Warner, who worked for him from 1900 to 1906, and Peter Hansen, who was with him from 1904 until 1909, when he left to work for Gustav's brothers' firm, L. & J. G. Stickley.

IN DETAIL : THE CRAFTSMAN STYLE

THIS HEXAGONAL Craftsman table from 1901 exemplifies Gustav Stickley's use of simple materials and straightforward craftsmanship. His durable, functional, unadorned furniture was balanced and interesting in its design. The strength of this and many other Craftsman designs flows from the raw geometry of their parts. In furniture that was undecorated, massive, and rectilinear, success depended on getting the proportions right.

A. *White oak is quartersawn to reveal dramatic ray fleck on the outer surfaces of the beefy legs. The great majority of Craftsman pieces were made with white oak, which was in keeping with the Arts and Crafts movement's preference for local materials.*

B. *Curves were used sparingly in Craftsman designs but to great effect. Like the corbels on a Craftsman settle, the arched skirts on this table lighten the severe geometry of the overall design.*

C. *The heft and plainly structural design of Craftsman furniture makes a visual link to house construction. Here, stacked cross-stretchers with an oversized locking peg literally tie the table together with an architectural flourish.*

D. *Craftsman furniture is not as strictly rectilinear as it appears at first glance. These legs, for instance, were given a subtle inward curve at the foot, which keeps them from looking like coarse planks.*

E. *Tusk tenons like these, used frequently in Craftsman furniture, give the piece a sense of strength and durability; they also serve an important decorative purpose in furniture that is otherwise nearly devoid of ornament.*

F. *Besides wood, Craftsman furniture used other plain and sturdy materials: leather, brass, copper, tile. Craftsman hardware was designed to add to the preindustrial-era flavor of the furniture. Metalwork generally bore hammer marks, reinforcing the impression of handcraftsmanship.*

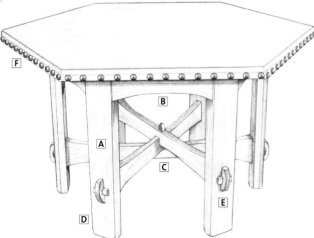

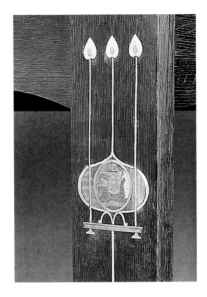

Harvey Ellis introduced a new vocabulary to the Craftsman line: thinned-down parts, occasional curves, and decorative inlay. With this hall table and armchair from 1903, he introduced a refined, feminine element to the raw and powerfully masculine Craftsman line.

Ellis drew inspiration from C. R. Mackintosh, among others. The inlay Ellis designed for his hall table, top right, and in the detail above was a direct translation of custom hardware Mackintosh created for his linen press of 1895, below.

Most prominent among Stickley's designers was Harvey Ellis, who worked for the company for less than a year before dying at age 52 in January 1904. In his brief time there, Ellis made a powerful and distinctive contribution to the Craftsman line.

Stickley's Craftsman furniture was praised in its day for making a refreshing departure from the humdrum historic revivalism that was then so pervasive, but it also was often criticized for being clumsy and massive. Ellis would change that. Trained as an architect and influenced by the English designer C. F. A. Voysey, Ellis introduced a lighter note to the Craftsman line. Legs and other massive members were thinned, more curves were introduced, and overall, the furniture attained a more refined appearance.

Ellis pushed Craftsman furniture in a surprising new direction when he added elegant, Glasgow-style inlay to some pieces. Stickley had emphatically eschewed such embellishments, but the inlay worked well with Ellis's less massive version of Craftsman style, further lightening the look of the furniture and adding interest to large areas of plain, flat surface. These inlaid pieces represented Stickley's high end and were not produced in nearly the same volume as the rest of the Craftsman line.

Stickley's Impact

Stickley did not simply copy English ideas and designs. He adapted them to factory production, and this was perhaps his most important contribution to the movement. Other large-scale American furniture manufacturers may not have shared Stickley's interest in the philosophy of the Arts and Crafts movement, but they recognized the potential of his new designs. In 1900, when Stickley's first Arts and Crafts-inspired designs debuted at a furniture industry exhibition in Grand Rapids, Michigan, other manufacturers saw right away that these distinctive pieces would appeal to Americans. More important, they saw that these pieces, with their rectilinear shapes and absence of ornament, would be perfectly suited to mass production.

"The modern trouble lies not with the use of machinery but with the abuse of it . . . ."

Gustav Stickley, 1906

The Retail Race

Within a year or two, virtually every major furniture manufacturer had introduced a line of similar furniture. By 1908, some 150 manufacturers were marketing some form of Mission furniture.

The furniture mass-produced in Grand Rapids during this period was markedly similar in form and design to that being made in upstate New York. Showrooms were full of designs that were close copies of Craftsman furniture. But as Stickley's competitors warmed to the style, some variations began to appear. A handful of firms,

Stickley furniture at its most elemental is more an expression of structure than of style. This 1912 Craftsman settle is blunt, straightforward, and unadorned.

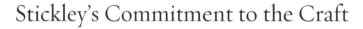

Stickley's brothers' among them, contributed some striking and innovative designs. The better designers with these companies reached beyond Stickley's forms and incorporated ideas from places as far flung as Vienna, Germany, and Belgium.

However, no matter what a design's pedigree may have been, it was invariably marketed under the banner "Mission."

Stickley's broadest impact, for better or worse, was through these scores of imitators in the furniture trade. A great many of these companies cranked out poorly made versions. Although Stickley wanted to spread the word about Arts and Crafts design and philosophy, he was incensed by the debased copies of his furniture, many of which were slapped together with dowels and then decorated with ersatz through tenons.

Stickley's Commitment to the Craft

Stickley's own furniture, always soundly made, reached quite a large public directly. After 1900, Stickley never again presented his Arts and Crafts furniture at a furniture trade show, preferring to display it at smaller, Arts and Crafts-themed fairs. He also sold it at his factory, through two Craftsman retail stores (one in Boston and one in Washington) and through 50 other retailers located throughout the country.

Stickley undertook another venture that was responsible for educating Americans as to the philosophical roots of the movement and the best examples of the style worldwide. This was *The Craftsman,* the monthly magazine he founded in 1901.

In the course of its 15-year run, *The Craftsman* would publish the work of most of the significant Arts and Crafts designers in Europe and North America. It reached beyond furniture, embracing

Providing a window on 1910, this contemporary office is entirely outfitted with period Craftsman products, from the light fixtures and furniture to the rug and the burlap wall treatment. Assembled by an avid collector of Arts and Crafts furnishings, the office is located in a house built recently from plans drawn by Ellis.

architecture, ceramics, gardening, and a host of other crafts. It was a highly respected forum where prominent architects and designers traded ideas. The Arts and Crafts movement's unified approach to home design was reflected in drawings and photographs depicting cozy interiors with furniture, tile work, ceramics, fabric, glass, and architectural detailing all executed in Arts and Crafts style.

The Craftsman also was a canny marketing vehicle, educating the public and designers so they would better appreciate the context and quality of Stickley's own Craftsman furniture.

Gustav Stickley's The Craftsman magazine, published from 1901 to 1916, was one of the most important Arts and Crafts publications. More than a marketing device for Stickley, it featured articles by leading thinkers and designers, and was a cohesive voice for the American Arts and Crafts movement.

Which Is the Real Stickley Furniture?

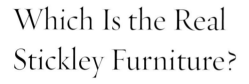

At the height of Mission furniture's popularity in the United States, four different U.S. companies working in the style could legitimately lay claim to the name Stickley. Gustav Stickley was the eldest of 11 siblings, and four of his brothers

Stout materials and strong joinery give Stickley furniture its rugged character. On this white oak Craftsman table from 1901, a leather top is secured with prominent tacks.

Stickley Brothers Co. borrowed freely from European Arts and Crafts designers. With delicate splayed legs and subtly arched aprons, this exquisitely proportioned drink stand shows that they created work on par with Gustav Stickley's best.

L. & J. G. Stickley's table and clock are right at home with the curtain and hall rug sold by brother Gustav. The clock is by designer Peter Hansen, who worked for Gustav before being hired by L. & J. G.

followed him into furniture making. In the 1880s, all five furniture-making brothers—Gustav, Charles, Leopold, Albert, and John George—worked together in a company called Stickley Brothers, which they founded in Binghamton, New York. By the 1890s, various brothers split off to form separate companies, working with and for each other in different combinations over the years.

When Gustav brought out his Craftsman furniture in 1901, his brothers followed suit. Within a year or two, all three of his brothers' companies were selling furniture that looked very similar to Craftsman pieces. The result is quite a challenge to the scholar or collector looking for "real" Stickley furniture.

Stickley Brothers Co. of Grand Rapids

In Grand Rapids, Michigan, the second incarnation of Stickley Brothers was founded in 1891. By the time Gustav's Craftsman furniture was launched, Stickley Brothers Co. of Grand Rapids, run by Albert Stickley, was a large company with a diverse product line. In its peak years, just prior to World War I, Stickley Brothers Co. employed some 300 workers and offered nearly 700 different designs in Arts and Crafts and other furniture styles.

Stickley Brothers Co. introduced its first line of Mission furniture in about 1902, calling it "Quaint Furniture in Arts and Crafts." Stickley Brothers Co. identified Scotland as the origin of this new style and gave a number of pieces Scottish names. This early Quaint style made considerably more use of decoration than Gustav's early Craftsman designs did. Inlay, marquetry panels, and carvings were employed along with amply sized hardware imitative of the Glasgow Style. Through decoration, Stickley Brothers Co. sought to relieve the severity and straight lines of Mission furniture.

In 1914, Stickley Brothers Co. introduced a line of Arts and Crafts furniture with a strong Austrian Modern influence. By this time, American manufacturers were having difficulty selling their heavy Mission lines. The new Austrian-inspired designs used lighter structural members, replaced solid-wood panels with lighter and cheaper caned ones, and employed little or no exposed joinery. Stickley Brothers Co. had some success with this line, but the end of the Arts and Crafts boom was approaching, and Stickley Brothers Co. was compelled to turn to other styles. The company continued to produce furniture into the late 1930s.

Stickley & Brandt

Located in Binghamton, New York, and run by Charles Stickley, the second-oldest of the brothers, Stickley & Brandt produced unremarkable furniture that was often directly copied from Craftsman and other Mission lines. For its Modern Craft line of furniture, Stickley & Brandt purchased hardware from the Craftsman Workshops.

Although Stickley & Brandt's designs resembled Gustav's, its craftsmanship did not. It employed a number of questionable cost-cutting practices, using thin shelf stock, cheap secondary woods, and false through tenons. Charles Stickley's most original designs, a series of settles and chairs with enormous, planklike front legs, were hardly elegant. Making no distinctive contribution to Arts and Crafts design, Stickley & Brandt was typical of many furniture manufacturers of the time. It ceased production in 1918, three years after Gustav Stickley himself declared bankruptcy.

L. & J. G. Stickley

Unlike their brother Gustav, who was in business to sell a lifestyle along with his furniture, Leopold and John George Stickley were simply in business to sell furniture.

Leopold and John George joined forces in Fayetteville, New York, in 1901, and after a period of subcontracting for other manufacturers, began to produce their own furniture, which they sold under the name "Onondaga Shops." It was remarkably similar to Gustav's. Quite a few pieces were direct copies, and Leopold and John George borrowed more than simply designs from their older brother; they produced a catalog nearly identical to his, used similar marketing techniques, and even chose a shop mark—a wooden handscrew clamp—that looked very similar to the Craftsman compass.

Stickley & Brandt plank chair is an example of the designs it produced when it strayed from copying. Its cost-cutting construction techniques are typified by what appear from a distance to be through tenons on the leg post but are actually applied nubs.

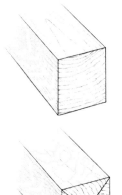

Quartersawn oak, with its lively flecked figure, was widely used in American Arts and Crafts furniture. L. & J. G. Stickley developed a method of gluing up posts from thin stock. This saved the expense of thick timbers and created a post with quartersawn figure on all four faces.

Focusing on market needs, L. & J. G. Stickley filled a niche that Gustav's higher-priced Craftsman line ignored. The company was quick to offer a number of small, inexpensive items such as side tables, simple chairs, and open bookracks—pieces that proved to be an ideal marriage of good design and mass production.

L. & J. G. Stickley furniture was stoutly built but not extravagant. Pieces would be joined with pegged tenons rather than the more costly through tenons that were a signature of Craftsman pieces. L. & J. G. Stickley also developed a clever method of gluing up thick legs and posts from thin stock, which cut costs while enabling them to display quartersawn figure on all four sides of a leg rather than on only two.

As the years passed, the company's design vocabulary grew. Its furniture began to incorporate influences from English Arts and Crafts, Glasgow Style, and Viennese Secession furniture. L. & J. G. Stickley also paid attention to developments that were taking place closer to home. In particular, the company watched

Small, less expensive items such as this book rack from about 1904 helped L. & J. G. Stickley expand their customer base.

the evolution of the Prairie School and the furniture designs of Wright. Later, it developed a very successful line of Prairie-style furniture of its own, characterized by the use of vertical spindles in rhythmic patterns. Pieces such as the L. & J. G. Stickley Prairie Settle capitalized on the power of a dominant horizontal line to convey a sense of strength and rootedness without using heavy structural members.

By 1910, Gustav's former employee Peter Hansen was L. & J. G. Stickley's chief designer. Meanwhile, Leopold was honing his sense of what the public wanted. The combination led to the company's Handicraft line, which sold well and made original contributions to the world of Mission furniture.

When the market for Mission furniture dried up at the end of the 1910s, L. & J. G. Stickley turned to making other styles. The company persevered, and although today it is no longer owned by a Stickley, it remains a force in the furniture industry. Under the ownership of A. J. Audi, L. & J. G. Stickley reintroduced a line of Mission furniture in 1989 that has contributed to the rebirth of Arts and Crafts furniture.

L. & J. G. Stickley was the only Stickley company to explore the Prairie style. This settle from 1913 was one of a series of successful designs adapted by L. & J. G. Stickley, and continues to be one of the company's most popular items.

The Stickley Family

THE BROAD POPULARITY that Arts and Crafts furniture achieved in America can be credited in good part to Gustav Stickley. In developing his Craftsman furniture, he applied his skills for mass-producing and marketing furniture to a modified version of the English Arts and Crafts aesthetic. When he did, a whole industry followed suit, and the vogue for simplified, solid, rectilinear furniture—the Mission style—was launched. Prominent among Stickley's followers were his four furniture-making brothers—Albert, Charles, Leopold, and John George. In various combinations, the Stickley siblings ran companies that made thousands of pieces of Arts and Crafts furniture. Much of it looked very similar to Craftsman furniture, although the quality was not always as high. There were variations, however, that introduced stylistic influences from other American and overseas designers.

THE BEGINNINGS OF THE CRAFTSMANS STYLE *are embodied in Stickley's drop-front Chalet desk. The lightness and stylized plant forms of his New Furniture are gone, replaced by unadorned, flat planes and straight lines. When the Chalet desk first appeared in 1900, it had curved feet and decorative cutouts. Stickley was quick to simplify his designs, and in this 1902 version the feet were straight tapers and the cutouts had been eliminated.*

STICKLEY'S CELANDINE TEA TABLE *was part of the New Furniture line that he introduced at the Grand Rapids furniture exposition in 1900. With its floral imagery, the table bears a resemblance to the furniture that Buffalo, New York, designer Charles Rohlfs was making at the time. Stickley would shed the curvilinear elements when he created his Craftsman line the following year.*

GUSTAV STICKLEY

After a career spent providing furniture in a range of historical styles, Gustav Stickley made a break with the past when he introduced his radically simplified New Furniture line in 1900 and his Craftsman line a year later. Craftsman furniture was notable for its plainness but also for its extensive use of exposed joinery and hammered hardware. Over the decade and a half that the Craftsman Workshops were in business, its designs were continually refined but remained essentially true to their original spirit.

ANOTHER FORERUNNER *of the Craftsman style, Stickley's hexagonal taboret of 1901 retains some embossed floral decoration on the top but otherwise is all straightforward practicality. The powerfully rectilinear and utilitarian Craftsman pieces soon erased the memory of Stickley's brief flirtation with curvilinear forms and decoration. In 1906 he wrote, "Anyone who starts to make a piece of furniture with a decorative form in mind, starts at the wrong end."*

THE NEW FURNITURE LINE *reflected many ideas Stickley had absorbed on a watershed trip to England and France in 1898. His Tom Jones drink stand bears evidence of English derivation in its lines as well as in its name, which is presumably drawn from the carousing title character of Henry Fielding's 18th-century novel.*

"My way of working is just a long series of personal discoveries."

James Krenov, 1976

GUSTAV STICKLEY ACHIEVED *pleasing designs through the use of proportion and strategically placed joinery details. In this double-door bookcase, a soothingly repetitive front grid of glass panes and two plain plank sides establish the mood of the piece. The only flourishes are found at the top and bottom of each side, where prominent tusk tenons cinch the piece together. The well-shaped pegs announce handwork and strength just where it is needed.*

TRADITIONAL TUSK TENONS *provide a link to the past as well as a powerful locking mechanism.*

JOINERY DETAILS ARE SUBTLE *and diffused over the piece on Gustav Stickley's writing desk from 1901. Repeating vertical grooves unite the paneled areas, and the many mortise-and-tenon joints only quietly announce their presence, just breaking through the surface. On the front posts, the through tenons alternate from front to side to front again, an arrangement that is structurally sound as well as visually interesting.*

THE REFINEMENT AND DELICACY *Harvey Ellis brought to Craftsman furniture in his brief stint as a designer with the company is manifest in this writing desk. Ellis introduced inlay patterns to the robust Stickley palette, as witnessed by this desk's drop front. A trained architect, Ellis also lightened the structural elements of Craftsman furniture, increased the use of pronounced curves, and gave many pieces an architectural flavor.*

Two of Gustav's younger brothers, Leopold and John George, built a furniture-making facility in 1901 in Fayetteville, New York, only a few miles from Gustav's Craftsman factory in Syracuse. Within a few years they had developed a line closely modeled after Craftsman furniture. The work was well made and affordable. L. & J. G. Stickley generated some notable designs of its own, including pieces related to Frank Lloyd Wright's furniture.

IN THEIR FIRST TWO YEARS *in business, Leopold and John George Stickley built furniture for other companies, including Gustav's. They also experimented with designs of their own, such as this small table from 1902, and sold them under the name Onondaga Shops. By 1903 they would focus entirely on producing their own line.*

L. & J. G. STICKLEY RELIED *heavily on Gustav Stickley's Craftsman pieces when designing its own line of Mission furniture. The company's indebtedness is exemplified by this library table from its shop and the corresponding table from Gustav's Craftsman line, shown on page 103. L. & J. G. Stickley was not the only company imitating Craftsman work. Competition among the many firms producing Mission furniture was fierce, and shameless copying was widespread.*

WHEREAS GUSTAV STICKLEY'S *furniture, always very carefully made, was priced at the high end of the Mission market, L. & J. G. Stickley was attentive to the middle of the market as well. It made a wide assortment of small items—such as these taborets—that were within the price ranges of most middle-class homeowners.*

A MAGAZINE STAND *from L. & J. G. Stickley again demonstrates the company's readiness to supply smaller items to make a sale. Many companies worked the same territory, both stylistically and in terms of price, so that without a manufacturer's label, it is often very difficult to trace the origins of a piece.*

by L. & J. G. Stickley is a close copy of a piece made by Gustav Stickley which appears on page 97. Gustav was no stranger to imitation; the design of his table was lifted nearly verbatim from the English Arts and Crafts designer M. H. Baillie Scott. The table's stylistic origins lie in medieval furniture.

NOT ALL OF L. & J. G. STICKLEY'S designs were cribbed. This mouse-hole trestle table was an original design that was marketed in several sizes. The simplicity of the design and the prominence of the tusk tenons that secure the stretcher make this a classic of the Stickley style. The table is still being produced by L. & J. G. Stickley.

ALBERT STICKLEY

Albert Stickley's furniture firm, Stickley Brothers Co., was a prominent manufacturer in Grand Rapids when Gustav's New Furniture line was introduced at the city's annual exhibition in 1900. Like the other major manufacturers in town, Albert Stickley immediately recognized the potential of the new style, and he soon had his own Mission furniture in production. The quality of Stickley Brothers Co. designs was erratic, but over the years the company generated a number of noteworthy pieces, which drew from a broad palette of English and European sources.

BY 1904, WHEN THIS LIBRARY TABLE *was produced, Stickley Brothers Co.'s Quaint Furniture line had shifted. The exotic influences were stripped away to produce much plainer pieces. Gone were the fancy Scottish place names and the elaborate woodwork. This solidly constructed, rectilinear table relied solely on its hardware for decoration.*

THIS SETTLE FROM 1902, *with its elaborate, partially turned leg posts and carved center back slat, is an example of early Quaint furniture. To give the line a bit of an exotic air, each piece received a Scottish place name.*

STICKLEY BROTHERS CO. *furniture reflected the international currents flowing through the community of Grand Rapids. This desk, made for display at the Louisiana Purchase Exhibition of 1904 in St. Louis, features inlay and glass influenced by Japanese and English sources and also has* Jugendstil-*inspired hardware.*

© The Metropolitan Museum of Art,
Friends of the American Wing Fund (1992.90)
Photograph © 2002 The Metropolitan Museum of Art

AN EXPERIMENTAL ROCKER *demonstrates the latitude Albert Stickley allowed the Stickley Brothers Co. designers. His Quaint Furniture was unaffected by the ideological constraints that limited Gustav Stickley's Craftsman line. If Albert felt the need to change course quickly to improve sales, he would simply do it. Gustav, whose philosophy was spelled out clearly in* The Craftsman, *preferred not to tinker as much with his company's direction in design.*

STICKLEY BROTHERS CO. *used a variety of methods to reduce the heavy and rigid appearance of Mission furniture. In this armchair, the structural members are reduced in thickness and the back is fitted with a woven panel. Stickley Brothers Co. made extensive use of caned panels in its 1914 line of Austrian-inspired furniture.*

In 1904, when this piece was built, *a writing desk in the social room of a house was a status symbol. Fall-front desks, eminently presentable, offered a place to write without using up too much space. This pleasing and functional design was just one of many fall fronts offered by the Stickley Brothers Co.*

Refined and delicate, *a Stickley Brothers Co. hall chair from 1904 combines the Mission approach with an Austrian influence. Like many other manufacturers in Grand Rapids, Albert Stickley was continually investigating international trends and applying them to his furniture to make it appeal to as broad a market as possible.*

Handmade in a Factory

Mass Production in Grand Rapids

ANTI-INDUSTRIALISM was one of the primary forces that powered the Arts and Crafts movement. John Ruskin, William Morris, and many of the English designers who followed their lead bitterly criticized the dehumanizing effects of factory work on laborers and bemoaned the flood of shoddy products that were the result of such labor.

Nevertheless, the Arts and Crafts style was enthusiastically adopted by large-scale American furniture manufacturers. Ironically, in a number of cases factory-made products came as close as any to achieving the elusive Arts and Crafts dream of providing well-designed, well-made objects at affordable prices.

Furniture is fashion, and the great majority of American manufacturers viewed the Arts and Crafts movement as a trend rather than as a philosophy. The trend was powerful. More than 150 American factories produced Arts and Crafts furniture in the first 15 years of the 20th century. Some companies gave over their entire production to Arts and Crafts, but for many of them it was simply one of a number of furniture lines. Grand Rapids, Michigan, with the country's largest concentration of furniture factories, was a center for the Arts and Crafts style.

Most large American companies brazenly borrowed designs. Gustav Stickley's Craftsman furniture was the dominant style of the time, and many manufacturers copied it outright. The most innovative firms, such as Charles P. Limbert Company, drew design inspiration from abroad as well.

The unadorned Arts and Crafts style was an immediate hit with the public and was perfectly suited to machine manufacture. Through factory production, the movement's lofty ideals were watered down and made palatable for mass consumption, but in return the style achieved broad and enduring recognition.

Large factories produced the majority of American Arts and Crafts furniture. Much of it was uninspired, parochial design, but a handful of companies, such as the Charles P. Limbert Company, makers of this table, produced strong innovative designs based on international sources. This table is a close cousin to Mackintosh's oval-topped piece for the Willow Tea Rooms.

The Disappearing Artisan

WHEN PHILADELPHIA architect William Price decided to open a furniture shop at Rose Valley, Pennsylvania, in 1901, he looked for a few highly skilled cabinetmakers—and discovered that very few were left. The region, which had produced some of the finest furniture of the Colonial period, was becoming a town of furniture factories.

Furniture making in America changed dramatically in the 19th century. In the early 1800s, American furniture was still made one piece at a time in small, artisan-owned shops by skilled craftsmen.

By the close of the century, most furniture was churned out by the hundreds of pieces by semiskilled laborers in factories.

Surging Demand for Furniture

The transition was driven by rapid advances in machinery and methods of mass production, and fueled by a great surge in the demand for furniture. The population in the United States was booming, and as companies increased their scale of production, furniture prices declined and more people could afford to buy.

At the beginning of the 19th century, American furniture was all made by hand; by the end, it was nearly all made by machine. With its simple lines and lack of ornament, Arts and Crafts furniture was ideally suited to machine production.

Mission in the Midwest

Mission furniture was produced in shops big and small all over the country, but the engine of the industry was in Grand Rapids, Michigan.

Founded at the site of a trading post beside the Grand River in 1831, Grand Rapids had become, by the turn of the 20th century, perhaps the country's most influential center of furniture manufacturing. Other cities produced more furniture, but in Grand Rapids, furniture drove the economy and defined the city.

In the 1870s, Michigan's virgin forests were supplying half the American demand for lumber. Many of the logs were floated down the Grand River and sent through sawmills just above the rapids that gave the city its name. The ready supply of cheap lumber was a great advantage to the furniture manufacturers there and helped launch Grand Rapids toward its destiny as "the Furniture City." But the old forests were cut so fast that by the late 1880s the most prized hardwood species were dwindling, and so was Grand Rapids's competitive advantage.

The city's furniture-factory owners, already a tight-knit group, pulled together in the face of adversity. They decided to start a semiannual exhibition, the Grand Rapids Furniture Market, and within a few years it was attracting hundreds of exhibitors and thousands of attendees from around the country. Soon it became the premier furniture exhibition in the United States. With the attention came more commerce, and new furniture businesses moved in.

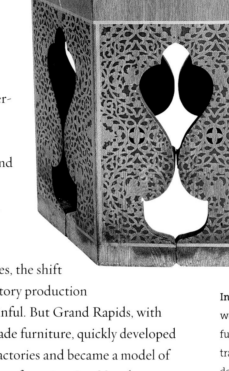

In older, Eastern cities, the shift from artisan shops to factory production was often halting and painful. But Grand Rapids, with little tradition of handmade furniture, quickly developed as a town of large-scale factories and became a model of mechanized furniture manufacturing. In 1880, the 15 firms producing furniture in the city employed nearly 2,300 workers—for an average of 150 in each factory. By 1905 the number of factories had more than doubled and the number of workers had nearly tripled—and there were nine factories that each had more than 400 workers.

Influences from around the world were expressed in Grand Rapids furniture. Large firms hired well-traveled designers. This taboret designed by David Kendall, with its Moorish influence, is evidence of his extensive travels abroad.

Grand Rapids companies absorbed domestic as well as international design trends. This chair from the Michigan Chair Company clearly draws its pedigree— and its unyielding ergonomics—from Frank Lloyd Wright.

"We have just completed our machinery for making Windsor chairs . . . so that we can almost . . . throw whole trees into the hopper and grind out chairs ready for use."
Ebenezer M. Ball, 1851

Because Grand Rapids manufacturers **churned out** inexpensive furniture, authenticity was less important than efficiency to them. A. Harry Sherwood developed a technique for rolling stain onto furniture parts, making plain pine look like more expensive quarter-sawn oak.

A Design Center Emerges

A rural city with such a strong culture of machine production would seem an odd place to find a thriving branch of the Arts and Crafts movement, which emphasized handwork. But as Grand Rapids was developing as a center of production, it was also developing as a center of design.

Competition among the many firms based there—and the many more that exhibited at the Furniture Market—was very strong. To gain an advantage, Grand Rapids firms began hiring well-educated designers from New York, Boston, and Europe. Staff designers were encouraged to travel, as factory owners often did, spending weeks at a time absorbing the latest styles in the decorative arts in England, Austria, and France. Within months of appearing in an avant-garde gallery in Vienna, a chair design might be reflected in the offerings at the Grand Rapids Furniture Market.

Whatever design inspirations were brought to Grand Rapids, they were always modified upon arrival and adapted for machine production.

A Journal Tells All

The Grand Rapids Furniture Record, founded in 1900, helped secure the city's position of leadership in furniture manufacturing and design. Like many of the city's companies, the *Record* embraced the Arts and Crafts movement.

Grand Rapids's position in the industry was further strengthened in 1900 with the founding of *The Grand Rapids Furniture Record.* A lavishly produced journal, it not only reported on the business of furniture manufacturing but also kept a sharp eye on trends in international furniture design. Other journals of the industry had been published in the last decades of the 19th century, but the *Record* quickly became the most vital publication for the American furniture manufacturer.

JOINERY IS at the heart of furniture making. Handcutting precise joints requires skill, experience, and time. The rise of machine manufacturing in the 19th century brought profound changes to furniture joinery. Machine methods were devised for making virtually all traditionally handmade joints. Factories also devised shortcuts for most joints, some of them structurally sound, some of them dubious. One quick way to assess the age and provenance is by looking at its drawer joints.

Manufacturing Joinery Methods

HIGH END

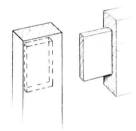

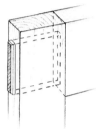

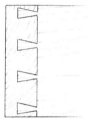

Mortise-and-tenon joint
Chairs and tables are essentially open frames, and for their rigidity they rely on strong joints where frame members meet. The mortise-and-tenon joint is best for frame joinery, providing wide, flat surfaces for gluing.

Dovetail joint
For drawer and carcase joinery, dovetails have been the state of the art for centuries. They provide ample glue surface and superb mechanical resistance to racking. Machine methods of cutting the joint were developed in the mid-19th century.

Through-tenon joint
The through tenon, in which the tenon extends right through the mortised piece to protrude on the far side, was a hallmark of Mission furniture. It was a handsome detail that proclaimed the strength and honesty of the construction. It also required a number of careful cuts, by hand or machine.

LOW END

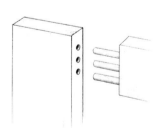

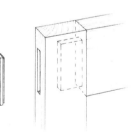

Dowel joint
Factories often used dowel joinery as a substitute for the mortise and tenon. It was much quicker to produce but with its limited glue surface was much quicker to come apart.

Lock-rabbet joint
In pursuit of a faster alternative to dovetailing, manufacturers developed the machine-cut lock-rabbet joint. Adequate only on very small, light-duty drawers, as in a jewelry box, it was used nevertheless on full-sized drawers, with predictable results.

False through-tenon joint
Some manufacturers came by their honest construction a bit deviously. The false through tenon gave the impression of a through tenon without the finicky fitting required by the real thing.

Development of Drawer Joinery

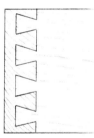

Hand-cut dovetails
With their narrow tails and irregular spacing, good hand-cut dovetails are more elegant and more interesting than their machine-cut counterparts. Even after machine methods had been developed for cutting them, dovetails on the drawers of the finest factory-made furniture were often cut by hand.

Machine-cut dovetails
The development of methods for cutting dovetails by machine was a breakthrough for large-scale furniture manufacturers. Machine-cut dovetails are as strong as hand cut, but technical constraints dictate fairly fat tails and a monotonous regularity in their layout.

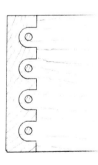

Cove-and-pin joint
Developed in the 1870s and used as a drawer joint by many manufacturers through the turn of the 20th century, the cove and pin was a machine-made alternative to the dovetail. Although not equal in strength, it was adequate and had a pleasingly decorative appearance that declared its machine origins.

Charles P. Limbert's European Influence

> *"When artists have been brave enough to depart from the use of ornamentation . . . their work has always met with success."*
>
> Charles P. Limbert Company catalog, c. 1910

The Charles P. Limbert Company produced some of the most striking factory-made furniture of the American Arts and Crafts movement. The company's furniture enlivened the Mission style with strong infusions of inspiration from C. R. Mackintosh and other European designers.

Charles Limbert learned the furniture trade as a salesman. He represented a number of different Midwestern manufacturers throughout the 1880s and 1890s, successfully representing as many as 18 companies at a time. He acquired a strong sense of design along the way, and when he started his own manufacturing business in Grand Rapids in 1902, his furniture was an instant success.

A New and Improved Plank

The earliest Limbert pieces, clearly influenced by Stickley's Craftsman furniture, employed massive structural members and stark basic shapes and relied on exposed joinery for occasional decoration.

With his 1905 catalog, Limbert introduced the furniture that would prove to be his most distinctive and enduring. Deeply indebted to Mackintosh's designs, the new work abandoned the massive posts of the Stickley style for plank construction. As Mackintosh had, Limbert learned to use negative spaces to give his pieces their presence, punctuating the planks with sharply defined geometric cutouts. The planks were often tapered, and curved aprons introduced an arcing line.

Several Limbert pieces are near copies of Mackintosh works. But Limbert wasn't simply a plagiarist; he elaborated on the themes from Mackintosh's furniture and developed a large, impressively cohesive line. Other American manufacturers often applied the same distinctive detailing to a range of pieces and called the designs a line. But Limbert's cutout pieces are thoughtful, balanced designs with their visual effects well integrated.

In addition to his Mackintosh-inspired line, Limbert produced much furniture in a style that combined Dutch folk and *Jugendstil* influences. The pieces are typically of plank construction with flowing curves and cutouts in naive shapes.

The best of Charles Limbert's furniture displays a clarity and lightness of form missing from much of Mission furniture. Limbert's cutout designs, like this oval table, were among his most successful.

Limbert's most powerful designs were a blend of the starkly simple and the sophisticated. This hall chair marries a medieval folk-furniture form—the plank chair— with tapers and trapezoids reminiscent of avant-garde Viennese designs.

Limbert ran a good-sized factory—with some 250 employees by 1912—and his pieces seem always to have been designed with machine efficiency in mind. The furniture was well made but generally included less of the time-consuming exposed joinery that characterized Stickley's Craftsman furniture.

The primary record of Limbert's thoughts on furniture is found in the essays that were printed in his catalogs. There Limbert convincingly laid out his belief in the basic Arts and Crafts tenets of honest joinery and simple, straightforward design. He also expressed his strong, somewhat quirky view that the origins of almost all good Arts and Crafts furniture could be traced back to Holland.

"True art in its simplest formula is simply use made beautiful."

Charles P. Limbert Company catalog, c. 1910

America's Dutch Infatuation

Limbert was of Dutch lineage. In 1906 he began calling his furniture Limbert's Holland Dutch Arts and Crafts. The same year, he moved his manufacturing plant to a new factory in the conveniently named town of Holland, Michigan, about 25 miles from Grand Rapids. After the move, the labels on Limbert's furniture carried

---

IN DETAIL : CORBELS

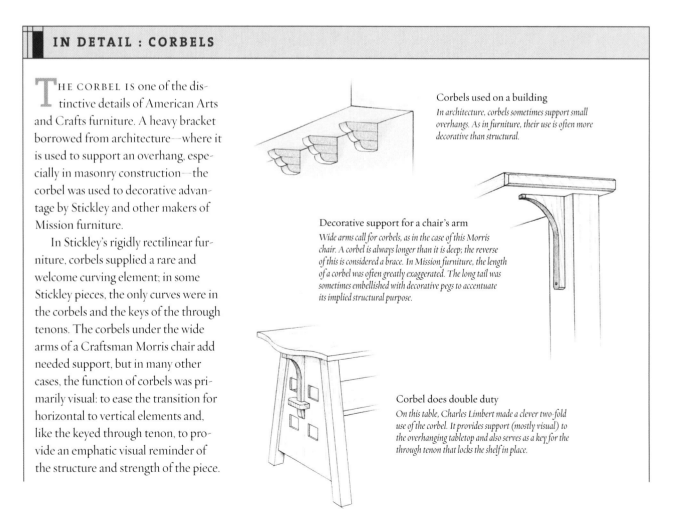

THE CORBEL IS one of the distinctive details of American Arts and Crafts furniture. A heavy bracket borrowed from architecture—where it is used to support an overhang, especially in masonry construction—the corbel was used to decorative advantage by Stickley and other makers of Mission furniture.

In Stickley's rigidly rectilinear furniture, corbels supplied a rare and welcome curving element; in some Stickley pieces, the only curves were in the corbels and the keys of the through tenons. The corbels under the wide arms of a Craftsman Morris chair add needed support, but in many other cases, the function of corbels was primarily visual: to ease the transition for horizontal to vertical elements and, like the keyed through tenon, to provide an emphatic visual reminder of the structure and strength of the piece.

Corbels used on a building
In architecture, corbels sometimes support small overhangs. As in furniture, their use is often more decorative than structural.

Decorative support for a chair's arm
Wide arms call for corbels, as in the case of this Morris chair. A corbel is always longer than it is deep; the reverse of this is considered a brace. In Mission furniture, the length of a corbel was often greatly exaggerated. The long tail was sometimes embellished with decorative pegs to accentuate its implied structural purpose.

Corbel does double duty
On this table, Charles Limbert made a clever two-fold use of the corbel. It provides support (mostly visual) to the overhanging tabletop and also serves as a key for the through tenon that locks the shelf in place.

Borrowing designs was standard procedure in Grand Rapids and throughout the American furniture industry. Limbert was a typically avid appropriator but was uncommonly good at choosing his sources. Limbert's best furniture is very deeply indebted to C. R. Mackintosh. Some pieces, like this café chair, left, were near copies; in other pieces, Limbert adapted Mackintosh's vocabulary of planks and cutouts to create a variety of new furniture forms.

Limbert Café Chair

Mackintosh Tea Room Chair

Two elements of Limbert's design repertoire meet in this cabinet. The straightforward, Stickleyesque character of some Limbert pieces is visible in the doors, but the piece is transformed by flanking bookcases embellished with tapered plank sides and bold cutouts.

Limbert's affinity for the deep tradition of Dutch fine art and furniture is evident in his company's furniture, its catalogs, and even in its name: Limbert's Holland Dutch Arts and Crafts. This lamp is one of a small number the company produced.

the line "Made in Grand Rapids and Holland" with no clarifying mention of Michigan after Holland. And in one catalog, an engraving of the new factory bears the misleading caption, "Our factory, which is located in Holland . . ."

America was enamored with Dutch culture at the time, a predilection evident in brand names and logos on products from Dutch Boy paints to Dutch cleanser. It's hard to know how much of Limbert's rhetoric was marketing and how much was conviction. He was clearly devoted to the Arts and Crafts movement—either because of a deep passion or because it was a successful business venture.

Limbert was unusual among Grand Rapids manufacturers in devoting his entire output to Arts and Crafts. When the market began to soften after 1910, he introduced a line of lighter pieces with caned panels which were still in the Arts and Crafts vein but represented a decided departure within the genre. By 1916, when it became clear that the marketplace had turned away from Arts and Crafts, Limbert began experimenting with other lines. He sold the company in 1921 after suffering a stroke, and died two years later. Arts and Crafts had been as good to him as he had been to it: He left an estate of nearly half a million dollars.

The wide variety of styles contained in Limbert's Arts and Crafts line included a series of pieces in which caned panels and thinned posts combined to create a lighter, Austrian-inflected version of Mission.

The Swedenborgian Church
was designed by Bernard
Maybeck and A. C. Schweinfurth.
Its exposed, rustic rafters, as
well as its chairs, were inspired
by Spanish missions.

Joseph McHugh's
Mission Furniture

Sometime in the mid-1890s, Joseph P. McHugh, who sold furniture and accessories
from his store, Popular Shop, in Manhattan, received a package from an interior
designer in California. Inside was a bold but simple chair with heavy legs, a plain
slat back, and a rush seat. The chair's design was inspired by chairs in the new
Swedenborgian Church in San Francisco which were said to be based on the crude
furniture found in Spanish missions on the West Coast. McHugh liked the design
for its roughness and its romantic associations with the frontier.

    The design also struck a chord with McHugh's clients. He put the chair on his
shop floor and it sold immediately. He had a batch of them made and they, too, went
quickly. By 1898, his catalog included a number of pieces dubbed "Mission" that
were derived from the Swedenborgian chair. Among them were several chairs and a

settee, their elements appealingly thinned down from the original chair but otherwise identical to it. By 1901, McHugh had a complete line based on the Swedenborgian design. He called it McHugh Mission.

Mission Appeal

The furniture was a success with the public and with other manufacturers, who began to copy it. The press took notice, too. The furniture was widely praised, attracting attention abroad as well as at home. One thing many writers seized upon was the name—and soon many manufacturers and consumers did the same. Within a few years, most American Arts and Crafts furniture was known as Mission.

From the start, people interpreted the name to mean that the new furniture had a mission: to reform the overwrought, overembellished styles then prevalent. And certainly many of the furniture makers whose work would come to be called Mission had just that in mind. But McHugh himself was more retailer than reformer. He used some Arts and Crafts rhetoric in his catalogs and advertisements but with far less fervor than competitors like Stickley and Limbert. And his furniture, although praised initially for exemplifying the Arts and Crafts ideals, regularly used false joinery and often compromised structural integrity to achieve its visual effects.

Designed in San Francisco in the mid-1890s and based on the simple furniture in West Coast Spanish missions, this chair from the Swedenborgian Church was the direct basis for Joseph McHugh's line of Mission furniture.

Joseph McHugh's version of the Swedenborgian chair is thinned and lightened. The design was so popular that McHugh soon created an entire line of furniture based upon it.

Armchair, 1896-ca. 1920m
Joseph P. McHugh & Co., white ash, rush, green stain, 36¹/₈x34¹/₄x 18¹/₄
Munson-Williams-Proctor Arts Institute, Museum of Art, Utica, NY (90.55)

At least three prominent makers of Mission furniture—Stickley, Limbert, and Elbert Hubbard—made it clear in print that they would prefer not to have their furniture called Mission. That was in part to distinguish their carefully crafted furniture from the mass of often poorly made copycats flooding the market under the name Mission. But at least in the case of Stickley, it may also have indicated a sense of rivalry with McHugh.

Who Founded Mission Furniture?

Stickley was often credited with originating the Mission style. This was no doubt due to the quality and purity of Stickley's furniture and to the personal prominence he gained through his magazine, *The Craftsman.* But Stickley's Craftsman furniture line debuted in 1901, at least three years after Joseph McHugh introduced his first Mission pieces. Although there is still some dispute over the matter, the name Mission seems to have originated with McHugh.

In a letter written in 1915, McHugh claimed that Stickley had made a few pieces of furniture directly from McHugh's catalog sketches when they first appeared, and had shown the pieces to McHugh. The story remains unconfirmed, but from the visual evidence it appears that Stickley may well have found some of the inspiration for his Craftsman line in McHugh's furniture.

"Mr. McHugh has dubbed his novel productions Mission Furniture. . . . We can only presume that the particular kind of mission after which this furniture is made is a mission of artistc reform and in no way connected with the ministry."

London Furniture Record, 1900

Joseph McHugh's Applied "False-Structural" Decorations

Two options for decorative bracing

On Joseph McHugh's furniture, what looked like structural cross bracing was often simply embellishment.

Factory Furniture

THE FURNITURE in this chapter shares a common thread: profit. Large-scale American companies were looking for something that would sell. They were attracted to the Arts and Crafts idiom because it had broad appeal and was easy to mass-produce. As a whole, the industry was conservative. The majority of furniture it turned out can be described as Stickleyesque: heavy, dark, rectilinear, and unadorned. Some companies simply made copies of popular designs by prominent manufacturers. But competition also bred innovation. Leading companies looking to distinguish themselves produced lines inspired by avant-garde designers ranging from Americans such as Frank Lloyd Wright and Charles Rohlfs to Englishmen A. H. Mackmurdo and C. F. A. Voysey, Scotsman C. R. Mackintosh, and Austrian Josef Hoffmann.

DAVID KENDALL, *chief designer for the Phoenix Furniture Company, did early, influential work in the Arts and Crafts style. His McKinley chair, first produced in 1894, has a starkness of line that prefigures the Mission style. With its square spindles and flat planes, it can also be seen as a precursor of Prairie-style furniture. It remained in production for 30 years.*

As a major center of production, Grand Rapids reflected the industry as a whole, turning out quantities of generic Mission-style furniture along with a range of more distinctive work enlivened by influences from the Prairie style to the Vienna Secession. Grand Rapids firms typically employed hundreds of workers, and all designs were adapted to manufacture by machine.

AN ANONYMOUS PIECE *made in Grand Rapids, this wall shelf gives evidence of a skillful designer who was well versed in the Arts and Crafts idiom.*

GRAND RAPIDS FIRMS *were nothing if not adaptable. This plain Grand Rapids cabinet is given an Arts and Crafts flavor with the mere application of elaborate hardware. With different hardware, the same piece might well have been marketed in a company's Edwardian or Shaker line.*

THIS HALL TABLE *from the Grand Rapids Bookcase and Chair Company possesses a European flavor, which is a departure from the company's straight-lined Cloister style. The thin top and shelf, along with the shallowly curved drawer fronts, stretchers, and corbels, give the piece a sprightliness seldom seen on Mission furniture.*

THE LUCE FURNITURE COMPANY *manufactured a broad range of furnishings in several period revival styles. During the Arts and Crafts's heyday, the company added a line of dining room and bedroom suites with a strong Glasgow-style influence.*

SOME GRAND RAPIDS MANUFACTURERS *added inlay to give their factory-made Arts and Crafts furniture the feeling of handcraftsmanship. The work was often subcontracted out to specialists, like the gifted Timothy Conti, who was responsible for this chair's inlay.*

MAKING A LATE ENTRY *into the market, the Grand Rapids Bookcase and Chair Company introduced its Life-Time line in 1910. Also marketed as "Cloister" style, much of the line was heavy, rectilinear, and unadorned, a fairly typical knockoff of Craftsman furniture. This gate-leg table shows a lighter touch.*

MANY PIECES *in Limbert's line were fairly straight adaptations of Craftsman furniture. This drop-front desk is a few degrees off the Stickley style. Handcraftsmanship is conveyed in the design through its hammered-copper hardware.*

ALWAYS AGILE IN RESPONDING *to trends in the market, Limbert introduced a line of inlaid furniture in 1905, just months after Gustav Stickley unveiled his Harvey Ellis-designed inlaid furniture. Neither of their companies did well with the labor-intensive work, so both discontinued production within a year.*

CHARLES LIMBERT
Charles Limbert's reputation rests primarily on his Mackintosh-inspired work, with its deft use of cutouts and negative spaces. His company, based in Michigan, also made furniture with a Dutch flavor. These plank-built pieces were enlivened by sprightly curves and naive motifs. In addition, Limbert produced many pieces of standard Mission furniture in the Craftsman manner.

LIMBERT'S USE OF OPPOSING *curves—from the forward-swelling feet to the long, graceful corbels and the shelf brackets—successfully enlivens an otherwise simple design. The transparent green stain was a popular alternative to fuming as a finish.*

LIMBERT'S FURNITURE *often possessed Mission's massive sturdiness but was softened by the frequent use of gently arching horizontals and long, tapering corbels. The curves gave some of his work a, Jugendstil appearance.*

OSCAR ONKEN

Oscar Onken was a successful Cincinnati manufacturer of picture frames and specialty furniture when he caught the Mission wave in 1904. Impressed by the European exhibits at the St. Louis World's Fair held in that year, Onken hired Hungarian Paul Horti to design for him. The resulting furniture, sold under the Shop of the Crafters label, was rectilinear in the Mission mold and distinguished by Horti's use of geometric inlays of wood and metal.

THE CINCINNATI-BASED *Shop of the Crafters' inclination toward Europe for stylistic inspiration is clearly embodied in this drop-front desk. It combines Jugendstil-like tapered and cutout planks with diamond-pane windows and wild grain, suggestive of Bavarian country furniture.*

INFLUENCED BY PROGRESSIVE *Austrian design, furniture made by Shop of the Crafters stands apart from run-of-the-mill Mission furniture. This chair was designed by Austrian Paul Horti. The same inlay panel integrated here was applied to virtually every item in Horti's line, resulting in some clunky pieces.*

JOSEPH McHUGH

Joseph McHugh was an importer
and interior decorator who became
acquainted with the furniture of the
English Arts and Crafts movement
before Gustav Stickley introduced
his Craftsman line. His McHugh
Mission line, produced in 1898,
anticipated the rectilinearity and
simplicity of Craftsman furniture
but not its massiveness. Some
of McHugh's pieces with the "X"
and branch motifs are among the
livelier pieces of American Arts
and Crafts furniture.

THIS MORRIS CHAIR, *one of McHugh's
most powerful designs, incorporates
the branching motif as a structural element
rather than as a purely decorative one.
McHugh's designer, Walter Dudley,
an architectural draftsman, may have
adopted the branching design from
half-timbering found on Tudor houses.*

McHUGH'S DESIGNS *were eclectic and
noticeably different. This drop-front desk,
with its no-frills construction methods, was
typical of his design vocabulary. No stickler
for honest construction, McHugh used ersatz
joinery for decoration and often simply
glued cross bracing to the surface of a panel
for visual effect.*

The Prairie School

A FRANK LLOYD WRIGHT house was not simply a shell to put one's things in but a fully elaborated environment whose every element was an expression of its theme. Wright and his Prairie School colleagues in the Midwest sought a complete marriage of architecture and decorative arts. For his Prairie-style houses, Wright typically designed furniture, carpets, lighting, stained-glass windows, hardware, and millwork. On occasion, he designed china and silverware to grace the dining table and, several times, a dress for the hostess. All of these ancillary designs were reflections or refractions of the forms, details, and materials of the house itself.

The Prairie house begat a distinctive style of furniture—rectilinear, planar, with minimal decoration and only rare traces of handwork. Not surprisingly, given its explicit links to the buildings for which it was designed, Prairie furniture often had an architectural appearance.

Because their furniture was intimately linked to the architectural scheme, Prairie designers were able to achieve unprecedented visual effects in an interior. But often, and especially in Wright's houses, the furniture related well to the house but less well to the user. As a result, Wright's furniture often lost much of its impact when it was removed from its original setting.

Wright and the Prairie School had strong roots in the Arts and Crafts movement. Their integrated environments were descendents of William Morris's Red House, in which many of the furnishings were also designed specifically for the house. And although Wright disparaged Mission furniture as "offensively plain, plain as a barn door," Mission's simplicity and rectilinearity make it stylistically comparable to much Prairie furniture. Wright broke sharply with the Arts and Crafts movement by rejecting handcraftsmanship as impractical, and designing his furniture to be made by machine. In spite of this basic disagreement, his work and that of the other Prairie designers were strong expressions of Arts and Crafts ideas.

Using shared forms and materials, Prairie School architects designed furniture, lighting, built-ins, carpets, stained glass, and wall treatments that blended to create beautifully integrated interiors. This room and its furnishings, designed in 1912 by the Minneapolis firm of Purcell and Elmslie for Purcell's own residence, embodies the Prairie School approach.

Arts and Crafts in the Windy City

CHICAGO, BIRTHPLACE of the Prairie style, was a scintillating city for an apprentice architect in the 1890s. In the years after the Great Fire of 1871 that devastated its downtown, Chicago rebuilt with big and beautiful structures. Powerful, pioneering buildings by such architects as H. H. Richardson, Burnham and Root, and Louis Sullivan rose one after another. The world watched as prominent architects competed to establish a style expressly suited to a new form: the tall building.

Chicago was also host at the time to another kind of ferment. It was a hotbed of Arts and Crafts ideas, influences, and experiments. On the West Side there was Hull House, established in 1889 to provide relief and education to the poor. Hull House was modeled after London's Toynbee Hall, which had ties to the English Arts and Crafts movement. Hull House served as a meeting place and catalyst for a range of Arts and Crafts programs, lectures, and organizations. Chicago was also home to the magazine *House Beautiful,* which began publishing in 1895; English Arts and Crafts designers were featured in the first issue, and the national magazine became a proponent of Arts and Crafts design. In 1897, Chicago was the second city in the country (trailing Boston by a matter of months) to establish an Arts and Crafts Society. Among its 150 original members was Frank Lloyd Wright.

Traditional in form, Wright's armchair from 1893, his first year in independent practice, appears to be modeled after H. H. Richardson's spindle-sided armchairs. Within two years, Wright's own more graphic, squared-off style would begin to emerge.

Frank Lloyd Wright, designer. Arm Chair, c. 1893, oak, 30¹/₄ x27¹/₄x37¹/₂ in., © Collection of the Frank Lloyd Wright Preservation Trust, Museum Purchase, 1989.56. 02 Photoghrapher: Phillip Mrozinski.

Louis Sullivan, Mentor to the Prairie School

In this atmosphere of cultural excitement, one figure stood out as a pivotal inspiration and influence for the whole generation of Prairie architects: Louis Sullivan. In a good building, Sullivan said, "form follows function," meaning that the use of a space should determine its shape. He called for an "organic architecture," or one in which all the parts and forms of a building were as closely and logically related as if they had occurred naturally. And although he himself trained at the Ecole des Beaux-Arts in Paris, where classicism was the reigning style, Sullivan eschewed traditional European forms in a quest for a new American architecture, specifically an architecture of the American Midwest. Although Sullivan rarely designed houses —the forte of the Prairie architects—and designed few pieces of furniture, his precepts played a prominent role in the development of the Prairie style.

Wright, who worked for Sullivan for five years and regarded him as his only equal as an architect, was the driving creative force behind the development of the Prairie style. But despite the aura of the lone genius that surrounded Wright, there were many others who helped him define and elaborate the Prairie idiom. When he was first in business for himself, Wright shared offices and ideas with a dozen other architects and draftsmen in Chicago's Steinway building. And when he moved his practice to his home in the suburb of Oak Park, he always worked with a staff of talented designers. Many of them went on to practice independently employing the Prairie vocabulary they had helped shape while working with Wright.

Louis Sullivan was not of the Prairie School, but he influenced it. This 1910 pierced wood panel from a table by Purcell and Elmslie demonstrates Elmslie's fluidity in adapting Sullivanian ornamentation to a Prairie setting. Elmslie, who worked for Sullivan for 20 years, had left his employ the previous year.

© The Minneapolis Institute of Arts. Gift of T. Gordon and Gladys P. Keith

Frank Lloyd Wright and the Organic Ideal

Geometry was at the heart of Wright's houses and furnishings. In common with his mentor, Sullivan, and in accord with Arts and Crafts practice, Wright depended on a close study of plants for the germ of his designs. Rather than adopting the fluid line of flora, he based his designs on geometric patterns abstracted from plants.

This practice evolved during the 1890s, reaching maturity with his first Prairie houses in the last years of that decade. Wright was seeking an original, native architecture. His buildings quickly became more purely geometric in form—their sides shed decorative ornament and their roofs were flattened. The buildings became

"It is quite impossible to consider the building one thing and the furnishings another . . ."
Frank Lloyd Wright

Where it all started. Wright designed this drafting table in about 1898 for the studio at his home in the Chicago suburb of Oak Park, Illinois. The stool and the table's base illustrate the rectilinearity emerging in Wright's designs at the time.

"I have seen buildings of Frank Lloyd Wright's that I would like to touch with the enchanted wand; not to alter their structure in plan or form or carcass, but to clothe them with a more living and tender detail."

C. R. Ashbee, 1911

lower and longer, hugging the ground with the horizontal emphasis that was said to reflect and respect the flatness of the Midwest's prairie landscape.

On the suburban streets where most Prairie houses were built, the new architecture looked unusual, nestled as it was between Tudors, Victorians, and houses in other standard European-derived styles.

Creating an Integrated Interior

Radical things were happening inside the Prairie house as well. Impatient with the formality and rigidity of the traditional interior, which he derided as "a collection of little boxes," Wright created flowing, undivided spaces.

To give definition and scale to these large, open rooms, Wright employed simple moldings on the ceilings and walls; patterns in the custom-designed carpets; built-in shelving, sideboards, seating, and storage; and suites of freestanding furniture designed specifically for the house, with each piece designated to stand in a specific spot. For some houses, Wright designed as many as 50 pieces of furniture.

Wright borrowed attributes of the building as he designed its furnishings. He put slab tops with long overhangs on sideboards and tables, mimicking his flattened roofs and creating a similar horizontal emphasis. Case pieces became flat sided, stark, and straight-lined. On chairs, rounded arms and legs yielded to right angles; round spindles were cut square.

Wright and the Machine

Many of Wright's beliefs and design practices corresponded with those of the Arts and Crafts movement. In 1897, Wright illustrated and helped hand-print a book called *The House Beautiful* in an edition of 90 copies. Wright was an admirer of William Morris, and the book was an undertaking in the mold of Morris's illuminated texts for his Kelmscott Press. Wright's reliance on local plant forms as the foundation of his designs is an echo of Ruskin's teachings as well as those of Owen Jones, from whose influential book *The Grammar of Ornament* Wright traced scores of designs as an apprentice architect. His drive to make the house and all its furnishings an integrated

Some of Wright's most powerfully graphic furniture designs were the high-backed dining chairs that developed from this one. Part of a set designed in 1895 for his own dining room, this chair originally had turned spindles. As Wright's pieces became planar, he replaced the spindles with square ones. In later versions, Wright extended the spindles past the seat to a stretcher below.

Frank Lloyd Wright, designer. Dining Chair, c. 1895, oak with leather, 57½ x18x19½ in., © Collection of the Frank Lloyd Wright Preservation Trust, Gift of Olgivanna Lloyd Wright, 1977.06. Photoghrapher: Phillip Mrozinski.

IN DETAIL : VISUAL ANATOMY OF THE PRAIRIE STYLE

THE PRAIRIE HOUSE and its furnishings were one organism. Just as the Prairie house was meant to grow out of its site, Prairie furnishings were meant to grow out of the architecture. Prairie architects took the forms, colors, and materials used in a house and applied them to the design of everything within it: built-in and freestanding furniture, carpets, stained-glass windows, light fixtures, murals, and hardware.

In the open-plan interiors pioneered by Frank Lloyd Wright and adopted by other Prairie architects, built-in and freestanding furniture helped modulate the space; strip moldings on the ceiling and walls were also used to give the open rooms definition. Molding and trim details used in the architecture were carried over into the furniture, which strongly affected the furniture's

appearance and form. The same wood used for wall and ceiling moldings—very often white oak in a species native to the site—would also be used for the furniture.

Prairie architects limited the use of freestanding furniture to what was absolutely required for comfortable living while incorporating built-in items wherever feasible.

design was shared by other Arts and Crafts architects from C. F. A. Voysey and C. R. Mackintosh to Greene and Greene.

But Wright broke sharply with Arts and Crafts ideology on the issue of machinery, and his views would influence the whole Prairie School. From John Ruskin forward, many Arts and Crafts designers disparaged machine production for the shoddy goods and degraded working conditions it created. Wright, however, saw machinery as the tool of the artist, and machine production as the inevitable way of the future. Resistance, clinging to an anachronistic idea of craftsmanship, he derided as wrongheaded and impractical.

His simplified, geometric designs were perfectly suited to machine manufacture. And machine production greatly reduced costs. Wright's ambitious interiors, full of custom designs, regularly exceeded their budgets as it was; very few of them would have gotten off the drafting table if the designs had called for elaborate carving, shaping, and hand joinery.

Relying on machines also meant retaining more design control. Wright expressed none of the usual Arts and Crafts sympathy for the creative needs of the craftsman and made no allowance for them. Using machines enabled him to keep craftsmen safely out of the design equation.

Flaws in Wright's Furniture

Wright was enormously prolific as a furniture designer throughout his long career, but furniture was never easy for him. He describes his early approach to chair design, for example, as "something between contempt and desperation." Even when his integrated interiors succeeded brilliantly, the individual pieces of furniture rarely stood up to scrutiny as separate works of the furniture designer's art. Even the strongest designs, such as his slatted, tall-back dining chairs, were weakened by an unfriendliness toward, almost a rejection of, the user.

The hard-edged geometry that served so well as the basis for his building designs proved too rigid for furniture. Writing in 1931, Wright gamely acknowledged that he found it difficult to "design furniture as architecture and make it 'human' at the same time. I have been black and blue in some spot, somewhere, almost all my life from too intimate contacts with my own furniture." Wright's furniture often has a strong visual impact, but upon close examination, much of it appears to have been both quickly designed and cheaply made.

George Mann Niedecken, Interior Architect

The studio that Wright ran in his Oak Park home from 1897 until 1909 was something more than an architect's office. Along with full-time draftsmen, there were in-residence apprentices, freelance designers, artists, and sculptors working collaboratively on Wright's ambitious projects.

George Mann Niedecken was one of Wright's most trusted associates. Trained in decorative arts in Chicago under Louis Millet (a friend and collaborator of Sullivan) and in painting under Alphonse Mucha in Paris, Niedecken came to Wright's attention for his talent as a painter. Their association began when Wright commissioned the 26-year-old Niedecken to create a mural for the Dana House in 1904. Wright was soon relying on Niedecken to produce presentation drawings and flesh out his concepts for furniture and interiors.

In 1907, Niedecken returned to his native Milwaukee to form a partnership with his brother-in-law, John S. Walbridge. Niedecken and Walbridge provided interior-design services for Wright and other architects while creating interiors of their own. Niedecken absorbed Wright's integrated approach to the design of an interior and became adept at conceiving and detailing furnishings that harmonized with a given house.

George Mann Niedecken helped define the role of the interior decorator, or interior architect, as he called himself. This space composed by Niedecken for the Adam J. Mayer House in Milwaukee in 1907 is a prime example of his talents. Responsible for the overall color scheme, wood trim, furniture, carpet, and recessed lighting design, he also conceived and painted the woodland mural above the fireplace.

RELATED ARTS & CRAFTS

Teco Pottery

Prairie architects often specified art pottery for their houses, and Teco was a favorite choice. The William Gates Pottery Co. of Terra Cotta, Illinois, introduced a line of earthenware vessels in 1901 named Teco after the town. The line emphasized glaze, architectural form, and affordability. The company relied on a molding process to mass-produce Teco pots, eliminating the expense and variability inherent in producing hand-thrown pots. The molding process lent itself to making pottery for the geometrically based Prairie house designs. The architectural look and low cost contributed to Teco's popularity with many architects and designers. Teco's emphasis on good design combined with mass-production methods had close parallels with the Wiener Werkstatte in Austria.

One of the many fruits of Niedecken's enduring collaboration with Wright, this dining table was made for the Irving House in 1909. As with much of the furniture Niedecken supplied to Wright, the authorship of its design is murky. In many cases, Wright provided a concept sketch and Niedecken fleshed out the design.

The Birth of Interior Architecture

Niedecken referred to himself as an interior architect and stressed that his goal was to design spaces that spoke the language that the architect had used in the building. In 1909, Niedecken and Walbridge opened their own cabinet shop so they could more closely oversee the production of furnishings.

When Wright left the United States for an extended stay in Europe in 1909, Niedecken assumed responsibility for completing the interiors of Wright's Robie and Coonley houses—two of his most important Prairie buildings. Niedecken not only executed the furniture designs that had been underway when Wright departed but also created other pieces from scratch.

After Wright returned from Europe, his practice faltered and he repudiated many of his former colleagues, whose Prairie-style practices were flourishing. But Wright continued to collaborate with Niedecken, using his services on a number of his last Prairie buildings.

Syncopated Ornament: George Washington Maher

"I believe sitting to be in itself an unfortunate necessity not quite elegant. . . ."
Frank Lloyd Wright, 1954

The call for a new American architecture was on many lips in the 1880s and 1890s. In Chicago, Sullivan expressed it most forcefully and influentially, but others joined the chorus. Among them was a young architect named George Washington Maher. Born in West Virginia in 1864, Maher apprenticed to a Chicago architect at age 13. He spent the next decade learning his craft before departing the office of architect J. L. Silsbee in 1888 to start his own practice.

At Silsbee's, Maher worked alongside both Wright and George Elmslie. All three young men were influenced by Silsbee's house designs, which were in the mold of H. H. Richardson's shingle-style houses. Maher's early independent houses also showed traces of the Richardsonian style. Silsbee designed furniture for some of his houses, and Maher went on to do the same.

in Oak Park, Illinois, in 1897, Maher's work here still shows a strong reliance upon historical European forms. Maher's motif-rhythm approach can be seen in the repetition of applied carvings on the sideboard, woodwork, and wall cabinets.

The Making of Motif-Rhythm

By the mid-1890s, Maher was beginning to develop a holistic approach to house and furnishing design that he called "motif-rhythm." Maher would choose a decorative theme for the house—a flower or an animal—and apply it in numerous variations to the furniture, built-ins, and other decorative objects as well as to the house itself.

Maher's furniture of the 1890s was characterized by a baronial massiveness. The motifs he used were naturalistic and deeply carved. By about 1904, under the influence of English and European Arts and Crafts designers as well as the Prairie

By 1908 a profound change had occurred in George Washington Maher's work—Prairie straight lines replaced heavy carving and historicism. The furniture still relied on Maher's motif-rhythm theory, but the motifs were now simply repeated geometric shapes.

"... the decoration of squares and geometric lines I find fussy and restless. But [Wright] has big ideas and is gloriously ruthless in sticking to what he believes."

Janet Ashbee, 1908

architects, Maher's houses and furnishings became sparer and more geometric. The furniture became lighter and the motifs evolved into abstract forms—squares, segmental arches, trapezoids.

Maher's motif-rhythm theory is analogous to Wright's practice of carrying a decorative theme throughout a house and its furnishings, but in Maher's hands the tactic was most often too literally employed, too predictable, and visually overwhelming. In Rockledge, the house in Minnesota that was Maher's magnum opus, for example, the rampant motifs are cacophonous rather than pleasing.

Prairie Partners:
Purcell and Elmslie

Of all the architects who worked in the Prairie idiom, the most prolific after Wright were the partners William Gray Purcell and George Grant Elmslie. In the 13 years of their partnership, from 1909 to 1922, Purcell and Elmslie built more than 70 Prairie-style buildings. Neither man had worked in Wright's studio, but their roots were intertwined with his nevertheless.

RELATED ARTS & CRAFTS

Built-In Furniture

Built-ins were a common element in the Arts and Crafts interior. Built-in seating, along with case pieces, reduced the amount of free-standing furniture in a room and created a more stylistically integrated interior. Architects from Hugh Baillie Scott to Charles and Henry Greene incorporated built-in items in their house designs, as did Gustav Stickley in his Craftsman houses.

Prairie School architects made the most extensive use of built-ins, designing inglenooks and window seats, built-in sideboards, beds, bureaus, bookcases, and cabinets. By echoing the forms, materials, and detailing of the archi-tecture, Prairie built-ins became extensions of the house itself. A band of stained-glass casement windows in an exterior wall, for example, might share its overall pattern as well as its glass detailing with a run of glazed cabinet doors in a built-in bookcase. By using the same moldings, materials, and sight lines on the freestanding furniture that they used on the built-ins, Prairie School architects created interiors in which all the furnishings were of a piece.

For some Prairie architects, a passion for fully original and integrated interiors was paired with a corresponding disdain for most other furniture. Wright, for one, liked built-in furniture for the control it gave him over the use of the space long after the client had moved in.

This bookcase from Wright's home and studio in Oak Park, Illinois, demonstrates how Prairie architects used wall moldings to wrap right around a built-in case piece, binding it visually to the house.

Some of the most distinguished furniture produced by the Prairie School, these chairs and their table were designed by Purcell and Elmslie in 1910 for the Keith residence in Eau Claire, Wisconsin. After Wright and Mackintosh built their striking tall-back chairs in the late 1890s, many other designers explored the form.

© The Minneapolis Institute of Arts. Gift of T. Gordon and Gladys P. Keith

Elmslie, a Scot born in 1871, arrived in Chicago in the 1880s and apprenticed alongside Wright in the office of J. L. Silsbee. After Wright left Silsbee's to work for Adler and Sullivan in 1889, he convinced Elmslie to do the same, and the two young architects worked together there until Wright opened his own practice in 1893.

Elmslie took Wright's place as Sullivan's chief draftsman soon after Wright's dismissal for moonlighting. Elmslie stayed with Sullivan for 20 years, many of them very lean. Sullivan was a master of intricate ornament, and Elmslie developed an aptitude for ornament while working for him. In the last years, Elmslie is thought to have done much of the designing in Sullivan's name.

William Purcell, nine years Elmslie's junior, worked briefly for Sullivan in 1904. Purcell stayed in close touch with Elmslie afterward, often seeking Elmslie's advice and collaboration on designs for buildings and furnishings.

In 1909, Elmslie left Sullivan to join Purcell in practice in Minneapolis, and the two men quickly developed a close, collaborative style of designing that produced a string of impressive buildings. Their designs show a commitment to craftsmanship and a flair for the ornamental.

In Purcell and Elmslie's houses and furnishings, Sullivanesque ornament is simplified and incorporated in the planar, geometric surroundings of the Prairie interior. The adaptation worked exceedingly well, and some of Purcell and Elmslie's furniture designs and interiors stand with the best work of the Prairie era.

Prairie Arts & Crafts

THE FURNITURE OF THE Prairie School was distinct from most other Arts and Crafts furniture in several ways. Much Prairie furniture was designed to be made by machine and employed concealed joinery. Also, it was almost all site-specific; not just designed for a particular customer, but for a specific house and a specific room. Relating so strongly to the building it was designed for, Prairie furniture could be somewhat architectural itself. As much as possible, Prairie furniture was built-in; if freestanding, it related closely in form and detail to the built-ins as well as to other interior details of the building. Just as the exterior of a Prairie home grew from its setting, so the furnishings grew from the architecture.

THE ADJUSTABLE-BACK *easy chair, or Morris chair, was readily adapted by Wright to a Prairie form. This chair, from about 1904, was made by the John W. Ayers Co. of Chicago, one of a number of firms Wright used. Also from this period is a Tiffany lamp and Gustav Stickley table, along with a large Teco pottery vase.*

MADE TO STORE *and display large prints,*
Wright's unusual table is practical and
visually balanced. With both leaves flat, it
provides a large display area. With one leaf
propped against a wall, prints can be displayed
upright; closed, the piece presents a very
narrow profile and provides storage.

Frank Lloyd Wright, designer. Print table (open),
c. 1895–1905, poplar and pine, 48½ x44x26½ in.,
© Collection of the Frank Lloyd Wright Preservation Trust,
Museum Purchase from Nora Natof, 1995.01.
Photoghrapher: Phillip Mrozinski.

EMINENTLY SUITED *for machine production, this*
1904 design with its straight lines and simplified
joinery seems almost primitive. The way the front
legs are tucked inside the seat rails makes for a weak
joint, an example of Wright's tendency to finesse
the details of structural integrity.

Frank Lloyd Wright, designer. Slant-back Chair (open), c. 1904,
oak, 18¾ x14½ x40. in., © Collection of the Frank Lloyd Wright
Preservation Trust, Museum Purchase from Nora, Magmel
and Lloyd Natof, 1984.06. Photoghrapher: Phillip Mrozinski.

GEORGE MANN NIEDECKEN

Trained as an artist and designer of decorative arts, George Niedecken collaborated with Frank Lloyd Wright on the interiors and furnishings for a number of Wright's Prairie houses. Niedecken also worked with other architects and completed commissions on his own. Calling himself an interior architect, Niedecken prided himself on designing furnishings that integrated with the architect's scheme for a building.

A RECENT REPRODUCTION *of a George Niedecken display cabinet, this piece combines Secessionist to Japanese influences. The skeletal framework makes an architectural statement without using broad areas of wood that might interfere with the function.*

WITH A PAINTER'S SENSITIVITY, *Niedecken used color to link the parts of an interior. Here, the wall, upholstery, and carpet are in harmony. This easy chair, with its curves and slants, typifies Niedecken's efforts to make furniture that was inviting to the user.*

MADE IN FIGURED BIRCH, *this bookstand and its companion pieces on these pages are reproductions that were made recently by Leo Barton of Milwaukee. Niedecken's originals, designed for the Adam J. Mayer house in 1905, are on display at the Milwaukee Art Museum.*

George Washington Maher

Along with Sullivan and Wright, George Washington Maher strove to develop his own ideas for an original American architecture. Maher's motif-rhythm theory, which called for the reiteration of one or more central themes throughout a house, was his method of imposing visual and thematic unity on a building and its furnishings. Maher worked in a succession of styles but applied his motif-rhythm theory to each of them.

BUILT IN 1912, *this monumental armchair is typical of the furniture designed for Rockledge, the summer house in Homer, Minnesota, that was Maher's residential magnum opus. The house and its furnishings show the impact on Maher of English designers C. F. A. Voysey and Hugh Baillie Scott and of the Vienna Secessionists.*

A TALL CLOCK FROM ROCKLEDGE *mimics the architecture of the house. The segmental arch of the bonnet, the sloping buttress sides, and the small trapezoidal capitals on the columns were all details that Maher repeated throughout the interior and exterior of Rockledge. Although tall case clocks were an 18th-century furniture form, they were modified and carried into the 20th century by a range of Arts and Crafts designers—Maher, Mackintosh, Stickley, and Rohlfs among them.*

THE CARVED LION'S HEADS *and shields on these chairs from the mid-1890s were reiterated throughout George Maher's Pleasant Home, providing an example of his motif-rhythm theory in action. The heavy forms and naturalistic imagery of Maher's early furniture later gave way to lighter, more geometric forms and abstract motifs.*

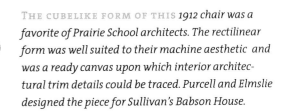

PURCELL AND ELMSLIE

The architectural team of William Gray Purcell and George Grant Elmslie, formed in 1909, built some 80 Prairie houses in less than a decade of active partnership. Elmslie, who joined Purcell after a 20-year career with Louis Sullivan, brought with him deep experience and a sophisticated sense of ornament and overall design.

THE CUBELIKE FORM OF THIS *1912 chair was a favorite of Prairie School architects. The rectilinear form was well suited to their machine aesthetic and was a ready canvas upon which interior architectural trim details could be traced. Purcell and Elmslie designed the piece for Sullivan's Babson House.*

© The Minneapolis Institute of Arts.
Gift of David and Patricia Gebhard

DESIGNED IN 1912 FOR *the Merchant's National Bank of Winona, Minnesota, this chair defines security and stability as clearly as the solid, blocklike architecture of the building. The chair's rhythmic spindle screen with repeating block inserts is its primary decoration. Purcell and Elmslie produced a similar chair for Purcell's own residence in Minneapolis, which was designed at the same time.*

© The Minneapolis Institute of Arts. Driscoll Arts Accession Fund

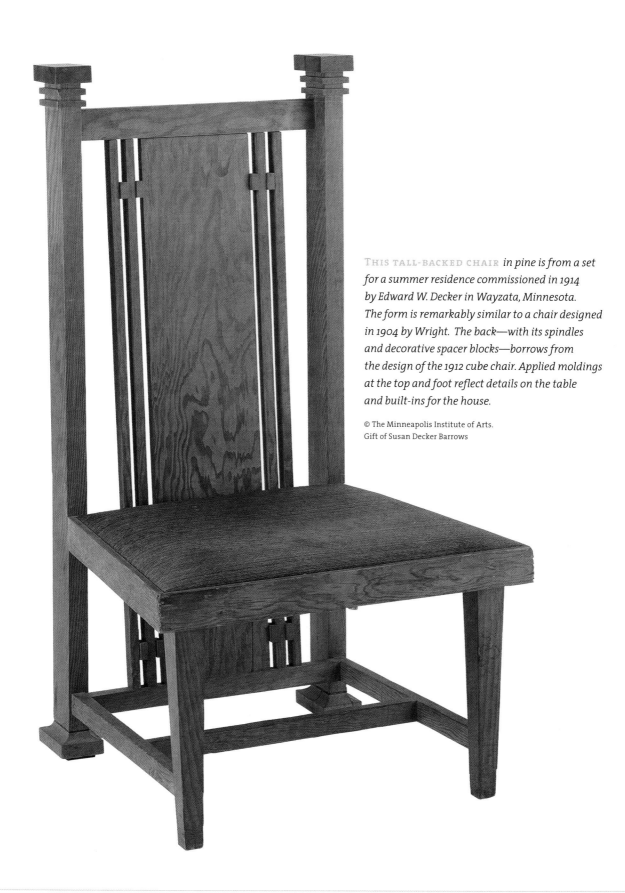

THIS TALL-BACKED CHAIR *in pine is from a set for a summer residence commissioned in 1914 by Edward W. Decker in Wayzata, Minnesota. The form is remarkably similar to a chair designed in 1904 by Wright. The back—with its spindles and decorative spacer blocks—borrows from the design of the 1912 cube chair. Applied moldings at the top and foot reflect details on the table and built-ins for the house.*

Utopian Communities

American Furniture and Social Reform

DOZENS OF TIMES in the course of the movement, in a wide range of ways and places, people attempted to use Arts and Crafts ideas to achieve social reform. They formed guilds, societies, settlement houses, cooperatives, colonies, and utopias.

In England, C. R. Ashbee's Guild and School of Handicraft was equally committed to training the urban poor in fine craftsmanship, and producing superb furniture and metalwork for sale. The venture was successful in both ambitions and lasted 20 years.

Grand Duke Ernst Ludwig of Austria, inspired by the furnishings and philosophy of the English movement, established a colony for decorative artists at Darmstadt. He wished to support excellent work and foster close relationships between progressive designers in related fields. The Darmstadt Colony made a stir in the design world but closed after four years.

America was richly endowed with Arts and Crafts communities. Three of the most interesting and most fully developed were Byrdcliffe, Roycroft, and Rose Valley. Byrdcliffe was Ralph Whitehead's colony for crafts and fine arts north of New York City. Roycroft was Elbert Hubbard's craft company outside Buffalo, New York. And Rose Valley was William Price's experimental community near Philadelphia. The furniture produced by these three communities was divergent in style, providing a reminder of just how broad a term Arts and Crafts is. And although Whitehead, Hubbard, and Price all drew many of their ideas for social reform directly from Ruskin and Morris, they applied the ideas so differently that the three communities were as dissimilar as the furniture they produced.

Utility and utopianism were blended in furniture built at a handful of Arts and Crafts communities. Elbert Hubbard's Roycroft in East Aurora, New York, was the most commercial of these, and the longest lived. The room at left is furnished with Roycroft peices.

Byrdcliffe's Aristocratic Utopia

ENGLISHMAN RALPH RADCLIFFE WHITEHEAD drank the Arts and Crafts elixir right at the source. At Oxford in the mid-1870s, Whitehead studied under John Ruskin. Before graduating, he traveled with Ruskin in Italy. In 1903, having moved to the United States with his American bride, Whitehead founded Byrdcliffe, a colony for crafts and fine arts based upon Ruskin's teachings.

The Byrdcliffe community was meticulously planned. Whitehead had been thinking for years about starting a colony. Having made several attempts, he was determined to succeed. Byrdcliffe's location, an idyllic hillside in the Catskill Mountains near Woodstock, New York, was chosen in part because it resembled Ruskin's favored Tuscan geography. Byrdcliffe's 30 buildings—including shops for woodworking, metalworking, and weaving; studios for painting and pottery; residences for craftsmen and teachers, and for the Whiteheads themselves; and a barn for the farm that would make the colony self-sufficient—were modestly sheathed with rough-cut pine and beautifully outfitted with the latest equipment and machinery.

Whitehead recruited a professor of art from Stanford to teach painting, craftsmen and carvers from the Boston Society of Arts and Crafts to head the craft shops. Various other writers, artists, musicians, and students joined Byrdcliffe in its inaugural summer. Furniture was to be Byrdcliffe's principal product, and Whitehead envisioned that, in time, sales would support the colony.

Blending Art and Craft

In Byrdcliffe's first several years, some 50 pieces of furniture were made, most of them bureaus and cabinets. The pieces were primarily rectilinear and restrained, with curved apron brackets and crown molding relieving their sternness. The few basic Byrdcliffe designs, closely modeled on English cabinets published in *International Studio* magazine, were made repeatedly. Although the forms were derivative, the furniture was distinguished by its decoration. Byrdcliffe artists and craftsmen painted the door panels

In its brief life from 1903 until 1905, the Byrdcliffe furniture shop developed a distinctive style, pairing plain cabinets with carved or painted door panels. Many of the panel landscapes, like this one by Herman Dudley Murphy, were painted in the moody style of Arthur Wesley Dow, who taught Murphy and some other Byrdcliffe artists.

of some cabinets with moody, soft-focus landscapes in the style of Arthur Wesley Dow. On other pieces, they carved the panels, creating stylized depictions of local flora. Framed by the solid and sensible but unremarkable cabinets, the panels created an appealing, original style.

The use of painted scenes, unusual in American Arts and Crafts furniture, was directly linked to the early furniture designs of Morris & Co., which were extensively painted with scenes from medieval history and literature. The connection to Morris was not coincidental: Whitehead had bought furnishings from Morris & Co. when he lived in Europe and brought them with him to America.

Byrdcliffe's shop was well equipped and the furniture produced was soundly made. This fall-front desk was built at the Byrdcliffe colony in 1904, in Woodstock, New York.

Byrdcliffe's furniture also reflected Ruskin's influence. The selection of common local woods—most often oak or poplar—was in accord with Ruskin's teachings, as was the depiction of local plants and scenes on the panels. In these and many other ways, Byrdcliffe was poised to succeed.

Utopia Meets Reality

But Whitehead's personality and his past were incompatible with a utopian future. The son of a wealthy manufacturer of piano felt, Whitehead was born to privilege and he was disinclined to relinquish it. As a young man, Whitehead had imagined socializing his family's manufacturing plant, but by the time he founded Byrdcliffe, Whitehead's youthful idealism had been tempered by bitter experience. "We are organizing," Whitehead wrote, "a life for a group of associated but independent

"Byrdcliffe is frankly a benevolent despotism. Whitehead is the absolute monarch, and no one is tolerated who is not in sympathy with his rule."

American Homes and Gardens, 1909

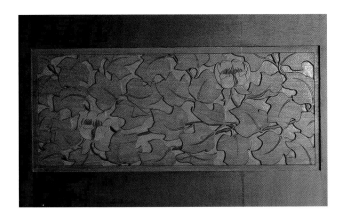

Acting on the teachings of Ruskin, Byrdcliffe artists incorporated images of local flora in their paintings and carvings for furniture. This panel depicts the leaves and blossoms of the tulip poplar tree.

Zulma Steele and Edna Walker, two painters who studied at Pratt Institute, designed many of the carved and painted panels on Byrdcliffe furniture. This unsigned rendering is probably by Steele or Walker.

Carefully relief-carved and then color washed and highlighted, these lily carvings add an organic touch to a rectilinear chest. The almost perfectly flat background was achieved with hand tools.

workmen in the country. We desire to form no 'community' because communities never have succeeded."

Although Byrdcliffe was imbued with the Arts and Crafts reverence for the sanctity of handwork, it was not to be a democratic workplace; Byrdcliffe was run as a feudal manor. Whitehead was accustomed to hiring musicians and actors to perform for him, and Byrdcliffe, it was soon clear, would be a similar proposition on a larger scale. Craftsmen and artists came and went at Whitehead's pleasure.

By the end of the first year, Hervey White and Bolton Brown, the two men who had helped Whitehead found Byrdcliffe, were gone. Others were recruited to replace them, but new hires would soon leave. Even those who remained in Whitehead's good graces would stay only for the summers.

White Pines, the Whiteheads's residence at Byrdcliffe, was, like all the buildings in the colony, built with plain materials in a relatively spartan style befitting an experiment in living a simple life.

Only about 50 known pieces of furniture were made at Byrdcliffe and very few of them found buyers. Most, like this cabinet, were still in White Pines when Ralph Whitehead's son Peter died there in 1975.

After Byrdcliffe's ventures in furniture and weaving failed, Ralph and Jane Whitehead took up pottery. This attic workroom still holds unglazed pots, molds, and jars of pigments for Ralph's experiments with glazes.

Byrdcliffe's Demise

The furniture shops, judged a failure, were closed in 1905. Whitehead, who had a distaste for the selling process, decided not to advertise the furniture, and most of it wound up lining the halls of his house, White Pines. Other factors may have contributed to its failure to sell—it was very expensive, and Byrdcliffe's remote location posed an unexpected challenge in getting it to market.

Whitehead shifted his attention and resources to the Byrdcliffe pottery, which lasted as a seasonal enterprise into the 1920s. Whitehead took up pottery himself, as did his wife, Jane. They set up a private studio in the family residence that produced a line called White Pines Pottery. But the pottery didn't turn a profit either, and Whitehead rented out various parts of the shops. Within several years of its promising start, Byrdcliffe became little more than a summer resort with crafts activities.

"We desire to form no 'community' because communities have never succeeded."

Ralph Radcliffe Whitehead, 1903

Elbert Hubbard and the Marketing of Utopia

Elbert Hubbard's Roycroft was the most commercially successful of all the Arts and Crafts communities. Begun in 1894, when he founded the Roycroft Press in East Aurora, New York, just east of Buffalo, the venture grew organically over the next half dozen years, with the addition of shops specializing in bookbinding, leatherwork, ceramics, art glass, metalwork, and furniture.

An encounter with William Morris in 1892 inspired Elbert Hubbard to found Roycroft Press in emulation of Morris's Kelmscott Press. The cabinet at right, a near copy of the one C. F. A. Voysey designed (see page 50), expresses Hubbard's debt to Morris.

"Am I a businessman? If so I am glad. . . . The World of Commerce is just as honorable as the World of Art and a trifle more necessary."

Elbert Hubbard, *The Philistine,*

In 1899, Roycroft had a workforce of about 50; 10 years later it employed some 500. In addition to the wide array of crafts it produced, Roycroft published two magazines—*The Philistine* and *The Fra*—filled with Hubbard's brand of homespun philosophy; a monthly pamphlet, *Little Journeys to the Homes of the Great,* containing an essay by Hubbard; and an assortment of books. Roycroft prospered under Hubbard's hand and even survived his death when he drowned on the R. M. S. Lusitania in 1915. His son, Bert Hubbard, stewarded Roycroft until it faltered in the Depression and he was forced to sell in 1938.

The Idealistic Businessman

Roycroft was a direct expression of Arts and Crafts ideals, but its success was due in part to Hubbard's readiness to compromise those ideals. Hubbard met Morris in 1892 and was deeply impressed with his talent, his philosophy, and most of all his

---

Mercer's Remarkable Tile

Henry Chapman Mercer, a Harvard-trained archaeologist, folklorist, and museum curator, founded one of the most successful and significant ceramic studios of the Arts and Crafts movement. His Moravian Pottery and Tile Works, established in 1898 in Doylestown, Pennsylvania, supplied decorative tile to architects. William Price used Mercer tile frequently on his buildings, including those he built for Rose Valley.

Mercer was exposed to Arts and Crafts ideas at Harvard, where he studied under Charles Eliot Norton, a close friend of John Ruskin and a cofounder of the Society of Arts and Crafts in Boston. Mercer stepped from scholarship to craftsmanship while studying Pennsylvania-

German redware, a folk pottery made with native clay. Discovering that redware was a dying craft, Mercer decided to learn its techniques himself. The experience ignited a passion for decorative tile making, and Mercer, spurred on by the poor quality of commercially available tile, chose to go into business.

Mercer made only hand-pressed tile, preferring its irregularities to the monotonous perfection of machine-made tile. A preference for handcraftsmanship was typical among Arts and Crafts designers, but Mercer was unusual in developing methods for making an affordable handmade product.

Moravian tile was also distinguished by its original palette of colored glazes. Mercer oversaw Moravian Pottery and Tile Works until his death in 1933. Although it's considerably scaled back from its heyday, it's in operation today.

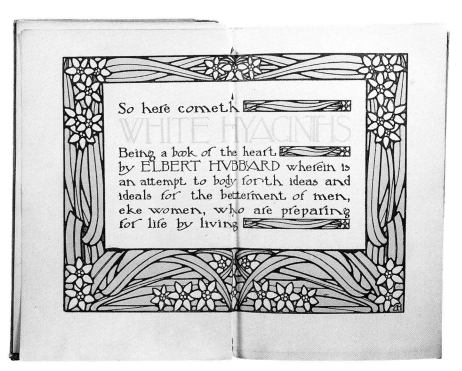

publishing company, Kelmscott Press. When Hubbard returned to America and founded his own press, it was very much in the image of Kelmscott. Morris's ideas and those of the Arts and Crafts movement were woven into many aspects of the Roycroft enterprise. But Hubbard's background was as a businessman, and his idea of utopia was a grafting together of a forward-thinking, paternalistic company on a standard American model and a community of craftsmen with an enlightened Arts and Crafts flavor.

Hubbard was 36 when he met Morris and had just abandoned a lucrative career with the Larkin Soap Company in favor of writing. At Larkin, Hubbard demonstrated a rare gift for marketing strategy. He originated the premium concept, shifted the company from a door-to-door sales business to a wholly mail-order one, and wrote highly successful advertising campaigns. All these techniques surfaced again at Roycroft, where Hubbard made a great success of selling crafts instead of soap.

Unremarkable Furniture

The furniture produced at Roycroft was one of the least remarkable things about the place. Hubbard himself was neither a craftsman nor a designer, and he never found a gifted designer for the furniture shop. Roycroft's glass and bookbinding departments were graced with the exceptionally talented Dard Hunter, and in the copper shop distinguished work was done by Karl Kipp. But Roycroft furniture,

ELBERT HUBBARD
(1873–1915)

Elbert Hubbard always drew a crowd. With shoulder-length hair and outfits worthy of Oscar Wilde, he cut a flamboyant figure. Hubbard was enormously prolific, and his writing always found a wide audience—in part by virtue of his verve as a writer, in part by virtue of his vigor as a salesman. Hubbard wrote much of the contents of *The Philistine,* his monthly mouthpiece from 1895 until his death in 1915. With a circulation of 200,000, it became the most successful of the many "little magazines" that flourished around the turn of the century.

Hubbard also wrote much of *The Fra,* a precursor to today's self-help magazines. Whether writing ad copy or an essay on spirituality, Hubbard's style was the same: an energetic, unpretentious, and playful blend of opinion, humor, observation, and exaggeration. He was also handsomely paid for his oratory skills and reportedly used lecturing as a way of raising money to fund Roycroft.

Roycroft books were designed, printed, and bound on campus. By 1901, the Roycroft print shop had more than 200 employees engaged in various aspects of the printing process.

No Arts and Crafts furniture manufacturer worth his salt would be without a Morris chair in his product line. Hubbard peppered the Roycroft catalog with several models. This one is a standard-issue Mission-style Morris chair with two twists: the use of maple, which lightens the look of a massive chair, and the Mackmurdo feet, which give it an English inflection.

although soundly made, was little more than a slightly altered reiteration of the Craftsman furniture that Stickley was producing a few hundred miles away.

The first furniture produced at Roycroft was reportedly built by carpenters to furnish the buildings they were erecting on Roycroft's quickly expanding campus. "They made the furniture as good as they could," Hubbard later wrote, and then "folks came along and bought it." Perhaps the carpenters had seen Stickley's furniture and figured it was a type they could easily make.

The Roycroft furniture shop was modest in scale, employing from six to a dozen workers at various times. It was well organized and equipped with modern machinery. Although the furniture's design was not outstanding, the pieces were made well and show evidence of careful handwork.

Roycroft's bookbinders developed exceptional skill with leather, and the furniture shops benefited from the expertise. This chair, with its hand-embossed upholstery, exhibits Roycroft's high standard of leatherwork. The chairs were listed in the 1906 Roycroft catalog for $125.

The Roycroft Brand

Hubbard took pains to distinguish his furniture from similar work, writing in the Roycroft catalog, "We would ask you not to class our products as 'Mission.' Ours is purely Roycroft—made by us according to our own ideas." But the main thing that distinguished Roycroft furniture from the mass of Mission furniture was the Roycroft orb-and-cross symbol or the Roycroft name, one of which was carved prominently on every piece.

Hubbard never missed an opportunity to advertise, and the prominent placement of the Roycroft logo was an early instance of branding. He was clearly selling the name Roycroft as much as the furniture. The Roycroft mark certified that the furniture was not churned out by an anonymous factory, but carefully made in accordance with Hubbard's homespun philosophy. Hubbard charged a much higher price for his goods and people paid.

Foreshadowing modern business practices, Hubbard relied on the strength of his brand to sell his products. The Roycroft name or orb-and-cross symbol was always prominent on the furniture.

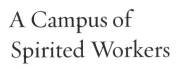

DARD HUNTER
(1884–1966)

Dard Hunter was 20 when he read about Roycroft in an issue of Hubbard's magazine, *The Philistine*. Hunter decided to attend craft courses at Roycroft during the summer of 1904, and Hubbard quickly spotted his talent. Hubbard hired him and sent him to New York City to study stained-glass design. When he returned to Roycroft after a two-month tutelage, Hunter was charged with designing the leaded-glass windows for the Roycroft Inn, then under construction.

A gifted designer and craftsman, Hunter was soon working in the glass shop. At the same time, he contributed to Roycroft's books and magazines, and in 1908, he designed the first cover for Roycroft's new magazine, *The Fra*.

Hunter traveled to Vienna in 1910 to attend classes in papermaking, bookbinding, lithography, and type design. Afterwards, he set up his own shop on the Hudson River just north of New York City and became a celebrated bookmaker. He was recognized as a world authority on papermaking and published many books on the topic.

Roycroft's many craft shops often worked in collaboration, as in the case of this lamp, which combines work in wood, metal, and glass. Hubbard encouraged the cross fertilization, urging Roycrofters to train in more than one discipline.

A Campus of Spirited Workers

Roycroft was built as a campus, with housing for some of the craftsmen, a farm supplying food, and a hotel for the many visitors it attracted. Life was enriched by regular concerts, communal walks, sports, picnics, and by lectures by Hubbard and by an impressive roster of prominent visitors. The pay was typically minimum wage, but working conditions were excellent by the standards of the time. Workers were trained in apprenticeship style and were encouraged to move from craft to craft.

Working at Roycroft was a long way from toiling in England's inhumane mills. And while all of this accorded with Arts and Crafts ideals, it was also the practice of Hubbard's former employer, the Larkin Soap Company. Hubbard, the idealist and businessman, remains controversial—disparaged by some for selling out the principles of the Arts and Crafts movement and praised by others for embodying them.

Rose Valley's Suburban Gothic

"After Roycroft furniture is installed in the home, the furniture question is settled."
Roycroft catalog, 1905

Some of the most extreme furniture to come out of the American Arts and Crafts movement was made in the first years of the 20th century at a small utopian community outside Philadelphia called Rose Valley. William Price, a prominent Philadelphia architect, founded Rose Valley and designed the furniture produced there in an uncompromising Gothic revival manner. Dark, somber, and extensively and expertly carved, Price's furniture seemed to bear no relation to the unadorned style of mainstream Stickleyesque furniture that defined the American Arts and Crafts movement in the public mind.

Close cousins of Stickley's Craftsman furniture, Roycroft pieces were almost never strikingly original. A few pieces were handsome, like this tall, trapezoidal bookrack, but most often the furniture designs were undistinguished.

Yet if Price's furniture seemed out of place with his contemporaries' Arts and Crafts work, it fit comfortably with the furniture and the ideas of the fathers of the movement, Pugin, Ruskin, and Morris, all of whom advocated a return to the values and the aesthetics of the early Gothic period.

Building a Way of Life

The plan for Rose Valley was twofold. It was to be a self-governing community where people of artistic temperament could live, owning their own houses but sharing Rose Valley's 80-acre property. And, like Roycroft, it was to be a cluster of workshops where groups of craftsmen would produce fine goods along Arts and Crafts lines. To finance the purchase of the land and the construction of the shops, Price secured a $25,000 loan in 1901. The shops were expected to generate enough income to repay the loan when it came due eight years later.

The first half of the plan was an immediate and lasting success. Price designed houses for himself and his partners, relatives, friends, and others who joined the community. From the first, Rose Valley was a congenial place to live, with its beautiful natural setting and handsome houses designed by Price, all within a short train ride of Philadelphia, where most Rose Valley residents worked. Informal plays, talks, and musical performances in the Rose Valley hall reinforced the bonds of family, friendship, and shared ideology.

Although out of step with the mainstream Mission style of Arts and Crafts furniture, William Price's Gothic revival work drew deeply from the tenets of the movement's philosophy and was firmly rooted in the medievalist aesthetic of Pugin, Ruskin, and Morris.

BUILDING THE BRYN ATHYN cathedral was one of the most remarkable and successful efforts to turn back the clock on the industrial revolution. Begun in 1913, it was a large-scale construction project where handwork was encouraged; a 20th-century job where Old-World skills were cultivated; an enormously expensive undertaking where craftsmen were made central to the design process; a job on which local materials were used and honest construction was stressed; and a true community of crafts where workers were formed into guilds with fully equipped workshops.

In all of these ways, the Bryn Athyn project brought to life the dreams of the many makers, writers, and orators of the Arts and Crafts movement. Yet the project was the building of a cathedral, and the motivation of the Swedenborgians who backed and built it was religious rather than secular. The simi-

When the Bryn Athyn cathedral was finished after 20 years under construction, Raymond Pitcairn kept the cathedral workshops busy building his own house, Glencairn, on property that abutted the cathedral site. This crib, with its highly architectural design, was built for Glencairn by Frank Jeck.

Typical of the methods followed in the project is this elaborately carved cabinet made to house the Bible. It is the reverse of mass production. There are no two details alike on the cabinet, and the latitude to devise and execute the design rested principally with the craftsman.

larities were not mere coincidences. The Swedenborgian religion stresses free will, values the individual, and prizes usefulness—all of which correspond with tenets of Arts and Crafts philosophy, and are implicit in the medieval manner of building cathedrals.

Raymond Pitcairn oversaw the Bryn Athyn cathedral project. Pitcairn, a devoted medievalist, hired like-minded architect, Ralph Adams Cram. But the very thing that brought them together—a shared approach to building—would prove their undoing. Pitcairn wanted more and more responsibility to flow to the craftsmen; Cram wanted to retain control of his design. Pitcairn wanted every aspect of the job to be achieved in an organic manner, executed by workers living nearby. Cram was inclined to hire some con-

tractors in the traditional way. Before long, Cram was removed from the job. Under Pitcairn's direction, the cathedral project became just what he had hoped.

There were workshops for timber framers, stone carvers, woodworkers, stained-glass workers, and metalworkers. No commercial products were used. Every hinge and handle was forged in the metal shop. Every stick of furniture was made in the woodshop. Every stone was quarried locally and hand chiseled; every rafter was cut from a tree felled in the surrounding area.

Like the cathedral itself, the furniture produced on the Bryn Athyn project was strongly influenced by Swedenborgian beliefs. But as nearly entirely handmade objects whose final appearance was deeply affected by the decisions of the craftsmen, they stand as well for the principles of the Arts and Crafts furniture maker.

Carved geometric and decorative patterns on this chair are continually transformed from panel to panel, symbolizing nature's infinite variety. Much of the Bryn Athyn cathedral's furniture is the work of a Czech-born cabinetmaker named Frank Jeck.

Meticulous and Masterful Designs

The second half of the plan, a range of workshops, was less successful. Furniture was Rose Valley's first product. For years, Price had been designing furniture for his architectural clients and having it made by Philadelphia craftsmen. With business flourishing, Price and his partner, Hawley McClanahan, decided to hire some craftsmen to make furniture for them full time in one of the Rose Valley shops.

The shop opened in 1901 as the houses at Rose Valley were being built, and over the next four years a half-dozen craftsmen produced some 500 pieces of furniture. Most of it was earmarked for Price's clients, but a small amount was sold through a showroom in Price & McClanahan's Philadelphia office.

Price's furniture was impressive, but it didn't make much of a commercial impact. Meticulously made and often involving masterful carving, the pieces were very expensive. Price was uninterested in advertising and never printed a catalog. When some notice was paid to the furniture after it was exhibited in St. Louis

---

IN DETAIL : VISUAL ANATOMY OF ROSE VALLEY GOTHIC

WILLIAM PRICE designed his Rose Valley furniture in a strict Gothic revival style that distinguished his work from his contemporaries' and linked it to the furniture of A. W. N. Pugin and the early work of William Morris.

A. *Tabletops were held in place by gravity with a few registration pins to keep the top from shifting. A customer had the option of ordering a more decorated top to use on special occasions along with a plain top for daily use.*

B. *Wedged tenons secured many of Rose Valley's pieces, making for easy disassembly. Price insisted on straightforward, honest joinery of the type favored by medieval joiners.*

C. *Unlike most Arts and Crafts work, Rose Valley furniture featured extensive pierced carving. In its joinery and finish as well as in its carving, Rose Valley furniture was made to high standards of craftsmanship.*

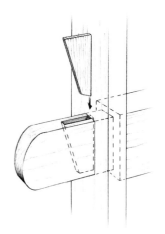

A secure joint was assured by seating a tapered wedge into a tapered mortise. The pressure of these faces against each other forced the tenon shoulders up against the leg assembly, making for a tight joint and a stable base for the table.

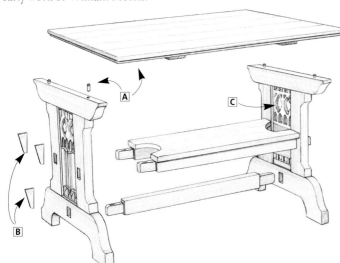

at the Louisiana Purchase Exhibition in 1904, Price turned away inquiries from customers who requested changes. For Price, the furniture was an expression of his beliefs, which couldn't be altered to suit someone's décor.

At various times, the other Rose Valley shops housed a pottery, a bookbindery, and a metalworks, but none was a full-time operation, and so the second half of the Rose Valley dream was not fulfilled.

Reaching the Intellects

Price, like so many designers of the movement, was nearly as inspired when using his pen at a writing desk as at a drawing board. Rose Valley's small magazine, *The Artsman,* launched in 1903, gave Price and others connected with the community a platform. Filled with passionate declarations of the Rose Valley philosophy and examinations of Arts and Crafts politics and aesthetics, *The Artsman* ran for four years, reaching an intellectual readership in America and England.

Price is said to have entertained dinner guests by reading from Morris's writings, just as Morris gave lively readings of Ruskin's prose. And Price's affinity for Morris was embodied in his plan for Rose Valley. Price modeled the community on a vision of the future depicted in Morris's utopian novel, *News from Nowhere* ("no place" being the literal meaning of utopia).

In Morris's book, set in the aftermath of a socialist revolution, people govern themselves through town meetings. The inhumane industrial economy had toppled, giving rise to pockets of skilled craftsmen. For a brief time, Rose Valley was host to such a pocket of craftsmen. But in 1906, finding the furniture shop a drain on his architectural practice, Price closed it for good.

The furniture built at Rose Valley received some acclaim but never grew into a viable business. The shops closed a few years after they opened.

William Price designed workshops and houses for Rose Valley. The original idea was to have craftsmen living and working there.

Utopian Furniture

ALL THREE OF THE UTOPIAN communities discussed in this chapter—Byrdcliffe, Roycroft, and Rose Valley—espoused a progressive social agenda that was tied directly to the precepts of the Arts and Crafts movement's founders, John Ruskin and William Morris. But the philosophy and the furniture produced at each of them are unique. The social and stylistic disparity among them was such that a person who felt comfortable at one of the communities would most likely have felt profoundly uncomfortable at the others. This diversity illustrates the extraordinary breadth of the Arts and Crafts movement.

AN EXCELLENT EXAMPLE *of Byrdcliffe furniture design, this imposing chest celebrates the beauty of nature and natural materials. The quartersawn white oak has been scraped and left unfinished. The superbly carved panels are attributed to Giovanni Troccoli, who taught woodcarving for at least one summer at Byrdcliffe.*

Byrdcliffe's furniture shop was a short-lived experiment, lasting but three summers and producing about 50 known pieces of furniture. And Byrdcliffe was beset with problems that led to rapid turnover and disillusionment. Yet by blending borrowed designs for solid case pieces with paintings and carvings by talented artists and craftsmen, Byrdcliffe established an elegant and individual furniture style that is easily recognized and admired.

THE SIMPLICITY *of overall form in Byrdcliffe furniture created a plain canvas for decorative painting. The lily on this lamp stand was painted directly on the flat panel, with the details in different colors demarcated with a fine black line.*

WHILE STUDYING WITH JOHN RUSKIN *in Italy, Ralph Whitehead adopted the lily as his personal symbol. During the furniture shop's tenure at Byrdcliffe, the flower was often used as a decorative element. The lily on this side chair's back splat is relief-carved and highlighted with a color wash.*

COMPARED WITH TYPICAL *Byrdcliffe cabinets, this one features finer proportions and a more extensive use of molding. Zulma Steele's painting of Queen Anne's lace is unusual, too, for being realistic rather than stylized. The only known Byrdcliffe cabinet in mahogany, it was made in 1904, when it was priced at $120, a princely sum.*

BUILT WITH THE WOOD *of the tulip poplar tree and depicting its beautiful leaves and blossoms in a carved panel, this cabinet doubly expresses the Ruskinian directive to take inspiration from local plants. With its uncomplicated form providing a frame for fine carving, it is a prime example of the Byrdcliffe approach to furniture making.*

ROYCROFT

The Roycrofters' extensive line was consistent in appearance with most other American brands of manufactured Arts and Crafts furniture. Roycroft designs stood apart for one reason: the prominent hand-carved logo or shop mark. Elbert Hubbard knew that his limited production capacity could never compete with manufacturers. He relied on the knowledge that his clients would pay a premium for a recognizable name brand and the status attached to it.

BOOKCASES WERE A PROMINENT ITEM *in the catalogs of Arts and Crafts furniture makers. This carefully mullioned single-door bookcase provides an example of the fidelity to good workmanship that prevailed in the Roycroft shops.*

PLAIN, SOLID, SIMPLE. *Without a gifted designer in the furniture shop, Roycroft produced pieces that were competent in construction but rarely distinguished in design. The best Roycroft pieces, like this taboret with its slightly canted and tapered legs, modified the standard Craftsman-style.*

Roycroft was dedicated to the Arts and Crafts ideal of furnishing the entire interior. In addition to producing all the major categories of furniture, his woodshop made accessories ranging from cradles to gun cabinets and wastepaper baskets. Roycroft's copper shop made hardware for the furniture.

Although quartersawn white oak *is the wood most associated with American Arts and Crafts furniture, many manufacturers offered the public a choice. Roycroft usually listed prices for mahogany and ash as well as for oak and occasionally curly maple, as in this library table.*

ROSE VALLEY

Ornament was anathema to many American Arts and Crafts furniture makers. Yet William Price built his reputation upon the use of it. In Rose Valley's magazine, *The Artsman*, Price wrote that his use of decorative carving was closer to the intent of the founders of the Arts and Crafts movement than was the stripped-down style of so many of his contemporaries.

THIS ARMCHAIR, *with its intricate carving and precise joinery, clearly shows how dependent William Price was on skilled craftsmen. But machines were also part of the process. Articles in* The Artsman, *Rose Valley's journal, may have deplored the dehumanizing effects of industrialization yet made it clear that a machine could be used like any other tool to carry the craftsman's volition.*

LIKE A GOTHIC CATHEDRAL, *William Price's Rose Valley furniture blended the rugged and the ornate. In this double-back bench, the lacy pierced carving on the backs contrasts with the flat seat and the rough spiral fluting of the legs. The Rose Valley shop produced some 500 pieces of furniture in its three years of operation, most of it for Price's architectural clients.*

PRICE CONDEMNED AS A MARKETING PLOY *the plain severity of so much American Arts and Crafts furniture. His work was equally powerful in structure and honest in construction but included decoration. The elaborate carving of this library table, built by Price in 1904 for a Philadephia client, was a scalding rebuke to the mass of featureless mainstream Mission furniture.*

American Innovators

Among the many
American designers who
absorbed the Arts and
Crafts aesthetic, a handful
made furniture so power-
fully personal that it
became a distinct style of
its own. The brothers
Charles and Henry Greene
built houses whose
integrated furnishings,
fittings, and architectural
woodwork gave the
movement perhaps its
highest expression. This
inglenook is from their
materpiece, the Gamble
house, in Pasadena.

Originality and the integrity of the individual worker were cornerstones of the Arts and Crafts philosophy. But the story of American Arts and Crafts furniture was largely one of followers and factories. Scores of large- and medium-sized furniture manufacturers mass-produced and marketed an ocean of Mission-style furniture in the first dozen years of the 20th century. Even Frank Lloyd Wright's Prairie-style furniture, a highly original manifestation of the movement, was designed to be made by machine and imitated by a flock of other designers.

The American movement produced a handful of designers whose work was so individualistic that it spawned no followers and so technically demanding that it could only be built by skilled craftsmen.

Three of the most impressive of these Arts and Crafts innovators were Charles Rohlfs, who ran a small shop in Buffalo, New York; John Scott Bradstreet, an interior decorator, retailer, and furniture designer in Minneapolis; and the partnership of the brothers Charles and Henry Greene, architects in Pasadena, California. In each case, the furniture took a highly personal vision to an extraordinary level of refinement. Such work required an enormous commitment of time and skill in the workshop as well as of money and aesthetic sympathy on the part of the client.

By its nature, furniture like this could only be made on a relatively small scale, but the power of the work insures its lasting significance despite its limited quantity.

Charles Rohlfs
and the Decorated Plank

"If I make a chair, I am a chair."

Charles Rohlfs, 1902

Charles Rohlfs's signature style blended flowing, organic carvings, straight lines, and flat planes. His 1902 desk, a tour de force of carved and pierced panel work, is a testament to Rohlfs's inventiveness.

Mission and Art Nouveau furniture would seem to be impossible bedfellows. Mission, with its flat planes, right angles, and absence of ornament, was the antithesis of Art Nouveau, a luxuriating blend of sinuous lines, fluid forms, and elaborate ornamentation. Yet the two tendencies were married in the work of Charles Rohlfs. Combining pragmatic plank construction with extensive carved embellishment, Rohlfs produced some of the most memorable and original furniture of the Arts and Crafts era. The duality in Rohlfs's work—practicality overlaid with whimsy—was primary to its power, and he never regarded this combination as a contradiction.

Extremes are also evident in his biography. Born in Brooklyn in 1853, Rohlfs began exhibiting talents both practical and artistic as a boy. At Cooper Union, a school in New York City, he studied chemistry and physics but also ornamental drawing, and he was praised as the school's best draftsman. His father, a carpenter and cabinetmaker, died when Rohlfs was 12. Afterward, Rohlfs worked to support his family but also managed to continue his education.

By the time he was 20, Rohlfs had become a designer of cast-iron stoves and furnaces. He excelled at it, bringing a splash of artistry to a workmanlike craft. On and off over the next 20 years, Rohlfs held a variety of positions with stove companies. But all the while, his heart was pulling him in a far different direction. By his mid-20s, Rohlfs was acting in plays, and within a few years he was earning good reviews while touring cross-country with a noted Shakespearean troupe.

From the Footlights to the Workbench

When he was 31, Rohlfs married Anna Katharine Green, a novelist who pioneered the detective genre. Rohlfs quit the stage, in part to appease his wife's family, who disapproved of the profession. Around this period, Rohlfs began working wood. Like many a designer/craftsman since, Rohlfs made his first pieces to furnish his own house and received his first commissions from friends and acquaintances who had seen the furniture there.

When Rohlfs was offered a job as a designer and manager of a stove company in 1887 in the burgeoning industrial town of Buffalo, New York, the Rohlfses moved there. Before long, Rohlfs had set up a makeshift attic workshop—with a packing crate serving as his workbench—and was making furniture again. Through the 1890s, Rohlfs flirted with the stage again, but in 1897, at the age of 44, he decided to make a go of it as a furniture maker.

Except for what he might have learned from his father, Rohlfs was self-taught as a craftsman and furniture designer. His lack of formal training accounts both for his rudimentary approach to joinery—he often substituted plugged screws or metal brackets for traditional joints—and for his fearlessness as a designer, one whose carvings and cutouts could be over the top but always had a vitality and compelling strangeness all their own.

Stark Work in Upstate New York

In its underlying structure and use of oak and ash, Rohlfs's furniture shows an affinity with the work that emerged at about the same time from Elbert Hubbard's Roycroft shops, just a few miles outside Buffalo, and from Gustav Stickley's Craftsman workshop outside Syracuse, New York. It is unclear in which direction the influence traveled, but the similarities between the basic forms produced in the three upstate New York shops is striking. For Stickley and Hubbard, those basic forms were sufficient: The structure was the style. For Rohlfs, though, the Mission-style structure was an armature for highly sculptural decoration.

Like Stickley and Hubbard, Rohlfs was attracted to the ideals of the Arts and Crafts movement, but his interest in it was more personal and less commercial than theirs. Rohlfs embraced the idea that work ought to be a joy and that the craftsman ought to be creative. He agreed with the movement's rejection of mass production, both for its adverse effect on workers and on the quality of the goods it produced.

With little surface area to be carved on, this 1903 plant stand shows Charles Rohlfs employing shaping and cutouts to mimic his flowing relief carvings.

CHARLES ROHLFS
(1853–1936)

With his small shop, his commitment to one-of-a-kind pieces, and his self-image as an artist making furniture, Charles Rohlfs was a forerunner of today's studio furniture makers. Rohlfs was in his 40s when he launched his career in furniture, and he did so with little training, having spent the previous two decades as a stage actor and a stove designer. Yet within a few years, Rohlfs's unusual furniture, with its stout construction and whimsical embellishments, gained him international notice. Rohlfs's Buffalo, New York, shop bustled in the first few years of the 20th century, but the vogue for his work cooled by the end of the decade.

"The precious part of a product is the part put into it by the craftsman."
Charles Rohlfs, 1900

Details are the pride and hallmark of small-shop production. Here, the craftsman can express "the dignity of labor," a phrase frequently used by Rohlfs in lectures and interviews. Even the metal fittings were designed by Rohlfs.

Yet, he was more engaged by his work than by the movement's rhetoric. "Do not think I am a reformer," he told *Woman's Home Companion* in 1902, "just put me down as a man who loves his work."

Reputation on the Rise

By the turn of the century, Rohlfs was beginning to get noticed. An exhibition of his furniture at the Marshall Field store in Chicago led to an article on his work in *House Beautiful* magazine, and orders came in from across the county. A successful display at the 1901 Pan American Exposition in Buffalo attracted more clients for his unusual furniture and led to an invitation to participate in the 1902 exposition in Turin, Italy.

Rohlfs's work was very well received in Europe and his reputation kept rising at home as well. In addition to an increase in single commissions, he began receiving requests for suites of furniture for the houses of the wealthy.

Rohlfs developed a highly personal style, but he was always willing to build to suit a customer's taste. This plain sideboard in figured mahogany is evidence of Rohlfs's ability to accommodate.

He designed interiors for Adirondack camps, and was commissioned by businesses to provide furniture for offices and exhibition displays.

Rohlfs's business thrived in the first decade of the new century, and he and his staff—which ranged from five to eight craftsmen—produced a wide array of pieces, most of them one of a kind. If a customer asked Rohlfs to repeat a design, he would typically reinterpret the older piece, at least in the carving. Despite the extreme originality of his designs, Rohlfs was committed to practicality and the needs of his clients. If someone wanted a piece in a plain style, Rohlfs would oblige.

The demand for Rohlfs's work stalled after 1907, and he spent much of his energy in the next several years designing and furnishing a new house for his family. Rohlfs stayed in business through the teens, though he had little work. He closed his shop for good in 1922.

More a fantasy than a timepiece, Rohlfs's tall clock is utterly unconstrained by historical precedent. It was exhibited at the 1901 Buffalo Exhibition and now stands in the town hall of Clarence, New York.

John Scott Bradstreet: Fine Furniture on the Frontier

John Scott Bradstreet brought high culture to the frontier. Born outside of Boston, he moved to Minneapolis in his 20s and quickly made his mark. He was highly regarded as an interior decorator, and he was also an influential retailer, selling furniture and accessories along with crafts and antiquities from his international travels. But it was as a furniture designer that Bradstreet made his signal contribution to the Arts and Crafts movement. He often designed furniture for his interiors, making adaptations of period or contemporary styles or reproducing unobtainable antiques.

Although the furniture Bradstreet designed helped distinguish his interiors, none of it was particularly noteworthy in its own right until he developed the style he described as "jin-di-sugi," which was mined from his exposure to fine English and American antiques and from his explorations amidst the woodcraft of Japan.

"I consider your furniture, as designed and brought out in the "Jin-di-Sugi" finish, the most 'unique and artistic treatment of wood yet produced."

Louis Comfort Tiffany, c. 1910

Conventional in form except for the front legs and skirt, this storage cabinet from 1905 was in Bradstreet's own office for many years. The sliding door with hand-painted cedar panel might have been among the treasures Bradstreet brought back from Japan—or they might have been painted at the Craftshouse by one of Bradstreet's artists.

"[The Englishman] could not remember where Mr. Bradstreet lived, so I furnished it. 'Ah, yes,' he said, . . . 'Could he not get a much wider recognition in New York, for instance?' Undoubtedly he could; but, after all, I suggested, the place for a missionary was among the savages."

Perry Robinson, 1907

A Progressive Retailer

Bradstreet started out in Minneapolis as a furniture retailer. He had a small store of his own for several years and then went into partnership with businessman Edmund Phelps. The Phelps and Bradstreet store occupied six floors of a large commercial building and sold accessories as well as furniture. Some of the store's inventory reflected Bradstreet's appetite for the esoteric, but much of it was suited to far more conservative tastes. This financially canny mixture of the progressive with the mainstream and of furniture with accessories would characterize all of Bradstreet's subsequent enterprises.

In the 1880s, using the store as a base of operations, Bradstreet began to make a name for himself as an interior decorator. A talented designer with wide-ranging

---

RELATED ARTS & CRAFTS

The Influence of the Far East

As the doctrine of the Arts and Crafts movement gained followers in the United States through the 1890s, it blended with a vogue for Eastern arts and objects. Often called the "Japan craze," it affected a wide spectrum of society, reaching beyond the arts into politics and industry. Japan was seen as a "living medieval society," and many American designers looked to the pure, preindustrial art of Japan as a model for innovation and creative expression. The asymmetry of Japanese art and its sensitive portrayal of natural beauty inspired Americans such as Frank Lloyd Wright, Charles and Henry Greene, and John Scott Bradstreet.

tastes, Bradstreet explored a succession of styles. His best early interiors followed the vogue among progressive designers for Moorish décor— he hung lush fabrics and tapestries from walls and ceilings and combined Oriental carpets, pillows, and brass accessories to create an exotic environment.

The cultural and business elite in Minneapolis came to rely upon Bradstreet's skills and judgment. In addition to attracting many private clients, Bradstreet began to receive plum public commissions. The most important of these was the Minneapolis Grand Opera House, which he decorated in Moorish style in the late 1880s. The Opera House interiors impressed critics and earned Bradstreet national recognition.

Chinese-style carving and a Japanese surface treatment are applied to a conventional Western furniture form in these cypress chairs made in Bradstreet's Minneapolis workshop in 1905.

The Craftshouse

Bradstreet took annual buying and scouting trips, going to Europe and the Far East in alternate years. In London, Bradstreet kept close tabs on Liberty's; his own stores often mirrored Liberty's selection and presentation of merchandise. Bradstreet was also impressed by William Morris's Kelmscott workshops, and in the late 1890s he established a firm in Minneapolis that borrowed business and aesthetic ideas from Liberty and Morris.

IN DETAIL : JIN-DI-SUGI

THE UNUSUAL SURFACE treatment John Scott Bradstreet devised for his most distinctive furniture and paneling took its name—*jin-di-sugi*—and its character from certain timbers he had seen in Japanese temples. For special features of their buildings, Japanese temple carpenters sometimes used wood from cedar trees that had been submerged in water or muddy sediment for hundreds of years. The long burial darkened the wood's color, sometimes to black, and softened and abraded the spring wood in each of the cedar's growth rings, creating a deeply textured, driftwood-like surface. The Japanese called their unusual timbers *jindai-sugi,* or cedar of God's age.

Using recently milled cypress rather than long-buried cedar, Bradstreet developed methods for approximating the color and contours of the ancient finish. In his Craftshouse workshop, the wood was first scorched to degrade the spring growth, then wire-brushed to leave an intriguing, topographic surface. Bradstreet's craftsmen then carved Japanese-inspired low-relief designs into the wood. A dark wash stain followed the carving and the finish was complete. Where maximum strength was needed—as with chair legs—Bradstreet's craftsmen used oak or other open-grained hardwoods. When wire-brushed and stained, the oak was nearly indistinguishable from the cypress.

© The Minneapolis Institute of Arts.
Gift of Wheaton Wood

The result was The Craftshouse, a combination retail space and workshop that was a magnet for anyone interested in the decorative arts; it even became something of a destination for tourists. Situated in a house that Bradstreet extensively renovated and surrounded by Japanese gardens, The Craftshouse was filled with a blend of fine crafts, decorative arts both imported and home grown, and antiquities, all artfully arranged. The feeling inside was something of a cross between a museum, a fascinating private house, and an unusual store. It was a resounding success.

In addition to retail space, the building housed Bradstreet's office and a tower workshop where a team of as many as 80 craftsmen—mostly from Scandinavia and Japan—built Bradstreet's furniture, millwork, and accessories. It was from this workshop that Bradstreet's jin-di-sugi emerged in the early 20th century.

Bradstreet's jin-di-sugi combined a topographic, driftwood-like surface, inspired by special timbers in Japanese temples, with stylized botanical carving done in a Japanese manner. Bradstreet created whole rooms in jin-di-sugi, applying the evocative surface treatment and carvings to wall panels and ceilings as well as to furniture. In an intriguing pairing, Bradstreet used Queen Anne-inspired chair and table forms for some of his jin-di-sugi pieces.

In the decade before his death in an automobile accident in 1914, the usually accommodating Bradstreet pressed his clients to commission jin-di-sugi interiors. At the end of his long, varied career, he had found his voice and wanted to use it.

Arts and Crafts Climax: The Interiors of Greene and Greene

"The idea was to eliminate everything unnecessary, to make the whole as direct and simple as possible but always with the beautiful in mind as the first goal. . . ."

Henry Mather Greene, 1912

The refined and intimately tactile furniture designed by California architects Charles and Henry Greene is a long way from Stickley's massive and starkly functional Craftsman furniture. A continent and 20 years in age separated the Greenes from their eastern colleague. Their methods of creating and marketing their work were also divergent. Despite the disparities between the designers, however, one grew out of the other. If Craftsman furniture was the launching pad for American Arts and Crafts furniture, then Greene and Greene's mature work was the rocket at its apogee.

Raised in the Midwest and trained in architecture at M.I.T., the Greene brothers went west and set up their office in Pasadena, California, in 1894. In the first years of their practice, the Greenes neither designed nor provided furniture for

The smallest detail loomed large in the work of Charles and Henry Greene. The many light fixtures they designed are no less admired than their architecture and furniture. Like Rohlfs, the Greenes appreciated and understood the "dignity of labor" and the joy of handcraftsmanship.

EVOLUTION OF THE GREENE AND GREENE STYLE

REEVE HOUSE BUREAU

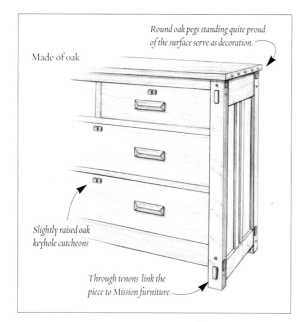

Round oak pegs standing quite proud of the surface serve as decoration.

Made of oak

Slightly raised oak keyhole cutcheons

Through tenons link the piece to Mission furniture.

An Early Affinity with Stickley

The Greenes' early furniture reflected their admiration for Gustav Stickley's Craftsman line. In this 1904 bureau from the Reeve House, the Greenes employed a heavy, rectilinear style not far removed from mainstream Mission work.

First Stirrings of a Personal Style

In overall format, this 1904 bureau from the Greenes's Tichenor House was similar to the Reeve bureau, but a few small changes radically altered its mood. A stepped design cut into the rails and drawer pulls lightens the piece and bespoke an interest in the Orient that soon transformed the Greenes's style.

TICHENOR HOUSE BUREAU

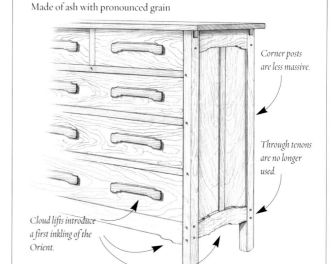

Made of ash with pronounced grain

Corner posts are less massive.

Through tenons are no longer used.

Cloud lifts introduce a first inkling of the Orient.

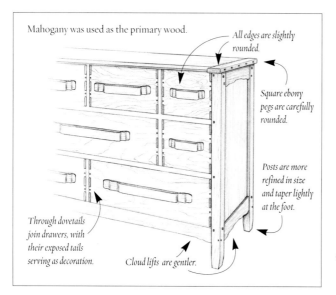

Mahogany was used as the primary wood.

All edges are slightly rounded.

Square ebony pegs are carefully rounded.

Posts are more refined in size and taper lightly at the foot.

Through dovetails join drawers, with their exposed tails serving as decoration.

Cloud lifts are gentler.

The Mature Greene and Greene Style

By 1908, when this bureau for the Gamble House was built, the Greenes's original and highly artistic style was fully developed. As their furniture became more sophisticated, so did the craftsmanship required to build it. The superb firm of Peter and John Hall produced most of the Greenes's demanding furniture.

GAMBLE HOUSE BUREAU

Compared with other Greene and Greene furniture of the time, this oak drybar with redwood panels is unusually restrained in its materials and detailing. Made for the Blacker House in 1907, the piece relies for its visual effect primarily on a fine sense of proportion—even the door hinges are graduated in size.

"It all started from my interest in Japanese early temple design. . . . In that simple timber work, they were the supreme masters."

Charles Sumner Greene

their interiors. It was only with the publication of *The Craftsman,* in 1901, that they saw furniture that seemed to them suited to their houses. Soon after receiving the first issue, the Greenes ordered Craftsman furniture for their Culbertson House. Inspired, they began designing their own furniture. And in these early pieces, the debt to Stickley is clear. Over the following decade, the Greenes's furniture designs underwent an extraordinary evolution, but even at its most refined and sophisticated, the work rested on the solid foundation provided by Stickley.

The Extremely Integrated Interior

In 1909, C. R. Ashbee noted that "like Frank Lloyd Wright, [Charles Greene] makes magic out of the horizontal line, but there is in his work more tenderness, more subtlety, more self-effacement than in Wright's work. It is more refined and has more repose." Ashbee's comparison of Wright's houses with those of Greene and Greene is particularly apt because the Greenes were perhaps the only Arts and Crafts architects who exceeded Wright in their commitment to design every shred of a house. Perhaps inspired by a series of articles in *The Craftsman* in 1903 in which Harvey Ellis advocated total design, the Greenes branched out from furniture and began providing designs for lighting, leaded and stained glass, hardware, and carpets.

Wright did the same, but his approach was in some ways the opposite of the Greenes's. In Wright's furniture, graphic impact often trumped functional concerns. In the Greenes's however, use and the user were always at the center of the design equation. Their preference for materials such as leather, mahogany, and

CHARLES SUMNER GREENE (1868–1957)

HENRY MATHER GREENE (1870–1954)

The brothers Charles and Henry Greene grew up in the Midwest, studied architecture in the East, and practiced their craft in the West. Although trained in the Beaux Arts tradition at Massachusetts Institute of Technology, they soon adopted the Arts and Crafts approach to architecture and furniture design. Infusing American Arts and Crafts furniture with an Oriental flavor, the Greenes created one of the most original and lasting contributions to the movement. The Greenes built their bungalows like handmade furniture, lavishing attention and craftsmanship on details from the copper gutters to the kitchen sink.

Finger joints used for their decorative impact were a common motif in the Greenes's furniture and in their architecture. In this writing desk, designed for a bedroom in the Gamble House, the drawers are finger joined. The Greenes used ash to make this desk and all the other furniture in the same room.

The Greenes's mahogany entryway bench was designed for the Blacker House. The seat bottoms lift to reveal storage bins, while the curved back slats have a springlike tension that invites one to lean back. Note the precise yet random pattern of decorative pegs at the crest rail joint.

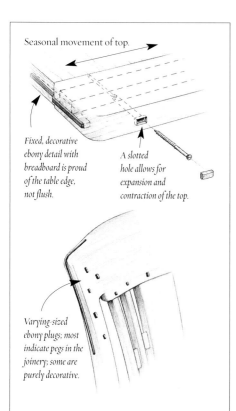

Seasonal movement of top.

Fixed, decorative ebony detail with breadboard is proud of the table edge, not flush.

A slotted hole allows for expansion and contraction of the top.

Varying-sized ebony plugs; most indicate pegs in the joinery; some are purely decorative.

The Greene brothers developed a decorative vocabulary for their furniture that was derived from its joinery. On pieces made in mahogany, they used ebony for splines and pegs, creating a rich contrast. Where two structural members met, they were often offset rather than made flush, emphasizing the intersection. The Greenes favored fingerjoints on drawers and small cases, and would leave the fingers proud to accentuate the rhythmic interlocking of the joint.

ebony and their use of eased edges, slightly offset surfaces, and proud polished pegs all arose out of an attempt to please the hand as well as the eye. And while Wright maintained his autonomy by designing furniture that could easily be made by machine, the Greenes depended on close collaboration with skilled craftsmen to get their furnishings made.

Greene and Greene in Asia

The evolution of Greene and Greene furniture was immeasurably aided by Charles Greene's affection for Japanese art and architecture and for Chinese furniture. When particular elements were first introduced to the Greenes's furniture—cloud lifts on bureau rails and drawer pulls, temple timber construction on table bases—their use could be slightly awkward, but the process of synthesis was quick. Within a few years, the Greenes's furniture seemed less a mixture of other accents than a strong voice of its own.

For the Greenes, as for Rohlfs and Bradstreet—and most other Arts and Crafts furniture designers—the period of greatest productivity ended before World War I began. Despite their youth and tremendous creative energy, and despite living into the 1950s, the Greenes never again approached the heights they achieved with the ultimate bungalows they built from 1907 to 1911.

After decades of neglect, the Greenes were honored as creators of "a new and native architecture" by the American Institute of Architects in 1952. But it would be another 20 to 30 years before the American Arts and Crafts movement would begin to stir again and the work of Charles and Henry Greene would be accorded a place among the movement's paramount achievements.

DIVERSITY IN DREAMLAND : CALIFORNIA ARTS & CRAFTS

DURING THE Arts and Crafts era, California was to the industrial Northeast what the Cotswolds were to London. Alluring for its landscape and for its lack of development, California attracted a wide range of artists and craftsmen. When English Arts and Crafts designer C. R. Ashbee visited the state in 1909, he judged that America's best work in the Arts and Crafts vein was being produced there.

The output of Arts and Crafts furniture in California was vibrant and extremely diverse. In San Francisco, Arthur and Lucia Mathews made furniture based on traditional forms vividly decorated with scenes and floral patterns drawn from the California landscape. The Mathewses' company, The Furniture Shop, which employed from 20 to 50 workers, opened in 1906, just after the great earthquake, and closed in 1920.

At the southern end of the state—and at the opposite end of the style spectrum from the Mathewses—was the architect Irving Gill in San Diego. Rather than looking to historical precedents in his work, Gill relied upon, as he wrote, "the source of all architectural strength—the straight line, the arch, the cube, and the circle." Gill's buildings and furniture often show a minimalist, proto-Modernist bent with an admixture of influence from the vernacular architecture of the West and Southwest.

This simple chair in redwood and cowhide is a reproduction of an Irving Gill design. It was made by Erik Hanson of San Diego.

Borrowing freely from classical architectural detailing, this drop-front desk is characteristic of the style of Arthur and Lucia Mathews. Function was never sacrificed in the Mathewses' designs no matter how elaborately decorated the surfaces.

© Oakland Museum of California, Gift of Margaret R. Kleinhans

Innovators in the States

The designers in this chapter are notable for the originality of their furniture. Each of them experimented with form and ornament to create highly expressive and extremely personal pieces. All these men were clearly aware of and influenced by the Arts and Crafts movement, but their own furniture reached well beyond the mainstream. Ideas from overseas inspired all of them. Charles Rohlfs traveled extensively in Europe; John Scott Bradstreet went on international buying trips each year and was particularly familiar with Japan; and the Greene brothers absorbed Japanese and Chinese aesthetics through lectures, museum shows, and international expositions. In each case, however, the external influences were folded into a personal vision, producing some of the most surprising and innovative furniture of the era.

WHEN OPENED, CHARLES ROHLFS'S DESK *is transformed. The dark-stained oak exterior reveals a precisely detailed mahogany interior and leather writing surface. Rohlfs often stained cabinet interiors a deep green.*

CHARLES ROHLFS'S TALL CASE CLOCK, *possessing one of the longest tenon pegs in all of furniture history, is an example of his willingness to flout conventional form for the sake of artistic expression.*

CHARLES ROHLFS

Charles Rohlfs's furniture is most often associated with the fluid, smoke-like carving that decorated a good number of his designs. His small shop, at times employing up to eight craftsmen, produced a great deal of work in its decade or so of peak operation. Rohlfs turned to furniture making in his 40s, but he quickly received acclaim blending rectilinear elements with beguiling curvilinear carvings.

THIS TRIANGULAR CANDLE STAND, *at 18 inches high, was one of a number of accessory items that Rohlfs offered his clients. The trademark carved surface treatment combines with the pierced panels to create an unusual design. The square metal panel at the top is adjustable and served both as a windscreen and a reflector for the flame.*

ROHLFS'S ROCKER FROM 1899 *has a strong flavor of the Orient. He made a similar chair for his own house.*

JOHN SCOTT BRADSTREET

The contributions of John Scott Bradstreet of Minneapolis to Arts and Crafts design have been largely overlooked until recently. He, like Charles Rohlfs and the Greene brothers, catered to a high-end clientele who were often willing to experiment, allowing him to push the envelope of conventional Arts and Crafts form. Simplified, machine-friendly design for the sake of affordability was not his goal; instead he strove for distinctive designs in which the mark of the craftsman's hand was apparent everywhere.

THE LIVING ROOM *of the William Prindle House (1905–1906) is the most complete of Bradstreet's* jin-di-sugi *interiors still intact. Now at The Minneapolis Institute of Arts, it was built for the Prindles's home in Duluth. Along with many* jin-di-sugi *panels and items of furniture, including one of his famous Lotus tables, Bradstreet incorporated many items of Louis Comfort Tiffany's favrile glass into the décor. Tiffany and Bradstreet had a cordial relationship throughout their careers.*

© The Minneapolis Institute of Arts, Gift of Wheaton Wood

GREENE AND GREENE

The furniture of Charles and Henry Greene was a masterful mixture of Arts and Crafts and Far Eastern influences, and it was built to an extraordinary level of craftsmanship. The Greenes's finest houses—their ultimate bungalows—were not only fully furnished with custom pieces but were themselves built to a standard that matched the furniture. When Frank Lloyd Wright saw the work, he said, "I do not know how you do it."

TWIN BEDS IN THE GAMBLE HOUSE *master bedroom demonstrate Charles Greene's affection for asymmetry. The balanced spindles are brought to life with an infusion of asymmetric detailing.*

MADE FOR A GUEST ROOM *at the Gamble House, this maple desk has a delicate vine inlay on the legs and silver backboard. The small, compartmented stationery cabinet could be lifted off the desk and carried to one of the porches, where letters could be written in Pasadena's perfect climate.*

THE BLACKER HOUSE OF 1907, *one of the Greenes' largest projects, presents an interior composition where furniture, architecture, and decoration flow together. The dining room table and chairs shown here, recently made by Jim Ipekjian of Pasadena, are exact reproductions of the original pieces, which were sold in the early 1980s by a previous owner of the house.*

The Revival of Arts and Crafts Furniture

Six decades after Arts and Crafts furniture fell into disfavor, the style and philosophy behind it found new life. Once again large manufacturers and small shops began producing furniture in the Arts and Crafts idiom. The 1995 sideboard at left, by Kevin P. Rodel reinterprets the Mackintosh washstand shown on page 8.

B Y THE END OF WORLD WAR I, THE ARTS AND CRAFTS was in eclipse, one that would last some 60 years. But in the 1970s scholars rediscovered the Arts and Crafts movement, and by the 1980s collectors began to do the same. Arts and Crafts antiques, long subjected to ridicule and consigned to the attic and the barn (if not to the fireplace) were dusted off and brought to auction where they sold for thousands, tens of thousands, even hundreds of thousands of dollars.

In a cultural climate that had led a new generation of comfortable, educated youth to reject the values of industry and go back to the land, a wave of people applied themselves to reviving yet again the lost crafts of their ancestors. Handmade furniture was reborn, and many furniture makers chose not only the lifestyle of their Arts and Crafts forbearers but also the aesthetic.

Many shops began producing Stickley-based designs, and the style crept back into the mainstream. Some makers also explored the fringes of the Arts and Crafts movement, producing furniture in the styles of designers ranging from Charles and Henry Greene to C. R. Mackintosh.

The Arts and Crafts style and philosophy had fallen into such disfavor for so long that those craftsmen who participated in its revival were struggling in the dark. But there were isolated makers and designers who kept the techniques and traditions of the movement alive and carried them forward across the six-decade divide.

Today, a century after the original movement reached its maturity, Arts and Crafts furniture is being faithfully reinterpreted in a contempory context.

The Sudden Death
of Arts and Crafts

"Less is more."
Ludwig Mies van der Rohe, 1959

In 1915, Elbert Hubbard died crossing the Atlantic, a victim in the sinking of the Lusitania. A year later, Gustav Stickley's Craftsman empire crumbled, his magazine closed, and he entered a 25-year retirement. The brothers Greene built the last bungalows in 1909, and Frank Lloyd Wright abandoned the Prairie style, with its roots in Arts and Crafts, soon thereafter. In Grand Rapids, the Arts and Crafts-based lines of furniture that had proliferated in the century's first decade were abruptly dropped in the second. And in Great Britain, C. F. A. Voysey's once-bustling career never revived after about 1910, and neither did Mackintosh's.

C. R. Ashbee, William Lethaby, and A. H. Mackmurdo had all turned to writing and teaching by the time the Great War arrived. The Arts and Crafts movement was essentially dead.

Meanwhile, by the 1920s, the modernist International Style, in many ways the antithesis of Arts and Crafts, was on the rise. Designers such as Ludwig Mies van der Rohe, Le Corbusier, and Marcel Breuer produced a purely functional style in architecture and the decorative arts that celebrated the rational efficiency of the machine and welcomed the use of industrial materials such as stainless steel, chrome, glass, and plastic to the domestic setting. The house, Le Corbusier announced, was a machine for living.

When the Arts and Crafts movement died, much of its ideology did as well. Its skepticism of the machine was replaced by a love affair with mechanization and technology. Traditional handcraftsmanship withered as machine methods and new materials were rapidly developed. The dignity of the worker was forgotten in the rush to factory production. The Arts and Crafts emphasis on the local, the personal, and the emotional were supplanted by the International Style's stress on the universal, the objective, and the rational.

The tubular steel structure of Ludwig Mies van der Rohe's elegant side chair from 1927 expresses the Bauhaus affection for industrial materials—a trend that helped spell the end for the Arts and Crafts movement.

The Aftermath in England

Despite the repudiation of the Arts and Crafts movement, a few craftsmen struggled to carry on its traditions. In England, the survivors were mainly from the Cotswolds, where life and craft had been most tightly interwoven.

Neville Neal, shown here in 1995, apprenticed with Gimson's chairmaker Gardiner and made turned chairs from Gimson's designs for half a century. In the late 1990s, he passed the business along to his son Laurence.

Ernest Gimson's legacy is particularly noteworthy. Gimson's furniture output had always been divided in two: There were turned, ladder-back chairs in the style of Gimson's mentor Philip Clisset; and there were case pieces, tables, and joined chairs. Remarkably, both sides of his oeuvre outlived him.

Gimson died in 1919, but his gifted Dutch foreman, Peter Waals, who had joined him in 1901, carried on the work of the shop until his death in 1937. Under Waals, the shop served many of Gimson's clients and employed many of his craftsmen. Waals, whose skills and sensibility had influenced Gimson's style, continued to build furniture to Gimson's designs and also produced some pieces of his own in a similar vein.

Gimson's ladder-back chairmaker, Edward Gardiner, continued building Gimson-designed chairs long after Gimson's death. Gardiner, a neighbor whom Gimson had recruited and trained to make chairs as a teenager, made these chairs through the 1950s, when he passed on his business—and all of Gimson's original chair patterns and templates—to his own apprentice, Neville Neal. Neal carried on the chair business in his tiny brick shop until the late-1990s, when he passed it along to his son Laurence.

The Barnsley Birthright

One of the most influential of the English craftsman survivors was Edward Barnsley. His career, which began in 1919 and lasted until his death in 1987, formed a bridge from the end of the original Arts and Crafts era to its rebirth more than half a century later. Edward was the son of Sidney Barnsley, who, in building each

"The old buoyancy is broken. . . . Gimson is dead. . . . the Daneway colony, like our Guild, is no more, except in each case for a few stragglers."

C. R. Ashbee, 1921

With a powerful graphic arrangement of drawers, this tall chest by Peter Waals represents the evolution of his own style, one strongly connected to Gimson's.

piece of furniture he designed, personified the Ruskinian ideals of pure handcrafts-manship, inspiration, and the merging of craftsman and designer. Edward's furni-ture, although rooted in the Cotswolds style, was often somewhat more delicate and attained in its maturity a Regency-tinged elegance. But each piece also exhibited an equal devotion to the principles of the Arts and Crafts movement.

The standard of craftsmanship set by Barnsley's shop was a beacon for other furniture makers. For the first 25 years, his shop operated with nothing but hand tools, as his father's had. And in addition to creating furniture of the highest quality, Barnsley's shop, with its tradition of rigorous craftsmanship, produced a number of sterling craftsmen who went on to careers as influential furniture makers and teachers.

Fifteen years after his death, the Edward Barnsley Workshop is still in business, building furniture to his designs and serving as an archive and study center.

Built in 1924 by Barnsley at the start of his career, this glazed cabinet in English walnut, with both Arts and Crafts and Regency influences, reveals that Barnsley was a highly accomplished designer and craftsman at an early age.

The Edward Barnsley Workshop has been an incubator of talented craftsmen and Arts and Crafts ideals for three-quarters of a century.

Danish Modern: Ruskin Revved Up

Hans Wegner's teak armchair illustrates the brilliant blend of modernist and Arts and Crafts sensibilities that characterized the highly successful Danish Modern furniture movement.

At the midpoint of the 20th century, while a handful of isolated craftsmen like Barnsley could be found quixotically making furniture in the Arts and Crafts tradition, a far different and more influential offshoot of the Arts and Crafts movement was blooming in Denmark.

There the International Style was grafted onto Arts and Crafts stock. Spare and functional, Danish Modern furniture owed a stylistic debt to talented Bauhaus designers such as Marcel Breuer and Mies van der Rohe. But these pieces were executed most often in solid teak or beech and finished clear to show the warmth and grain of the wood.

Designers in Denmark managed to solve riddles that had bedeviled Arts and Crafts designers since Ruskin called for the return of traditional craftsmanship—how to make something to a high standard of craftsmanship without making it prohibitively expensive; how to make something in numbers without losing the feeling of the hand-made; and how to make something in production without turning the craftsmen into factory workers.

Danish designers like Hans Wegner, well versed in the craft of furniture making, succeeded by working with relatively small shops and maintaining extremely close working contact between designer and craftsmen. Rather than simply handing over a drawing to be executed, Wegner was constantly present during prototyping and production so he could respond to any problems or opportunities that might occur as a new piece was being built.

In addition to being made in a way that honored the Arts and Crafts ideals of the sanctity of handwork and the interdependence of the maker and designer, Danish Modern furniture also happened to be beautiful, superbly well crafted, and quite saleable. Scandinavian furniture was popular among consumers worldwide in the 1950s and '60s and although its popularity diminished with the fading trend, its impact on the world of design remains significant.

The Dean of American Designer-Makers

Wharton Esherick's sensual yet functional furniture inspired many in the American craft revival—it was evidence that a furniture maker could also be an artist.

Wharton Esherick was the American analogue to England's Edward Barnsley. From the mid-1920s until his death at 83 in 1970, Esherick designed and produced handmade furniture that was highly distinctive and artistically expressive. For much of his career, Esherick was virtually alone in the United States in pursuing that path. In the 1960s and '70s, his example provided inspiration for many aspiring craftsmen in the revival of handmade furniture.

Unlike Barnsley, Esherick had no direct link to the furniture craftsmanship of the Arts and Crafts movement. Trained as a painter, Esherick quit that medium at 37 and turned to working wood: making sculpture,

Esherick's work begs to be touched. The wide chamfers, exposed joinery, and woven leather of this chair link Esherick's work to the Arts and Crafts movement.

wood-block prints, and furniture. Esherick did, however, have strong ties to Arts and Crafts ideas. He was involved for decades with the Hedgerow Theater at the Arts and Crafts community of Rose Valley. And in the early 1920s he and his wife lived at Fairhope, an Arts and Crafts-influenced utopian commune in Alabama.

Esherick's furniture was both sensuously sculptural and delightfully functional. It demonstrated for many aspiring American craftsmen the Arts and Crafts idea that a furniture maker could be as much an artist as any painter or sculptor.

Esherick's magnum opus is the home and studio he built on a hilltop outside Philadelphia in rural Paoli, Pennsylvania. Custom made in every detail—from coat pegs carved in the likenesses of the men who helped him build the house, to a freestanding spiral stair made of massive chunks of wood wedged into a twisting central trunk, to a kitchen floor pieced together from small pieces of wood rescued from the scrap pile—the building is a supreme example of the Arts and Crafts concept of the house as a fully intergrated work of art. Through his house, now open as a museum, Esherick continues to exert a strong influence on the field of studio furniture.

"If I can't make something beautiful out of what I find in my backyard, I had better not make anything."

Wharton Esherick

The English in America

By the mid-1970s, the growth of custom furniture making had created a demand for information about the craft. In the following years, numerous magazines, schools, and cooperative organizations were founded to serve the field.

Employing traditional craftsman-ship in the pursuit of a highly personal furniture style, James Krenov produced cabinets that had enormous influence on the rising generations of craft furniture makers in the last decades of the 20th century.

Among the most influential teachers were several with direct links to the Arts and Crafts movement. Ian Kirby and David Powell, English craftsmen who were veterans of the Edward Barnsley Workshop, both emigrated to the United States in the 1970s and set up schools to teach furniture making. Through the 1980s, Kirby Design Studios and Powell's Leeds Design Workshops trained several hundred Americans. Powell and Kirby both taught fundamental craftsmanship rooted in the expert use of hand tools.

Another alumnus of the Edward Barnsley Workshop, Alan Peters, a prominent craftsman with a shop in England has brought his version of the Barnsley message to America in a variety of workshops.

Krenov: The Articulate Cabinetmaker

Like the original Arts and Crafts movement, the American craft revival of the 1960s and 1970s was as much concerned with social philosophy and lifestyle as with aesthetics. And the man who most powerfully and appealingly described the life of a designer-craftsman was Swedish-trained cabinetmaker James Krenov. In a series of best-selling books written from 1975 to 1980, Krenov articulated his highly personal approach to making furniture. Many readers credit Krenov's books with having altered the courses of their lives.

RELATED ARTS & CRAFTS

Arts and Crafts Reenters the Mainstream

Large-scale American manufacturers participated in the revival of Arts and Crafts furniture just as they did in the original movement. As prices for Arts and Crafts antiques rose through the 1980s and more and more small shops began building furniture in the style, companies gradually entered the arena as well. In 1989, the L. & J. G. Stickley company, which had long since moved on to making furniture in a variety of other styles, reprised a line of Arts and Crafts furniture. The Thos. Moser Company introduced a line of Craftsman-influenced furniture in the same year. And by the mid-1990s, even such mainstream companies as Ethan Allen and various department stores were featuring furniture in the Stickley style.

Krenov's books depicted a dreamy but uncompromising pursuit of self-expression in wood. His approach propounded the dignity of handwork, the unity of art and craft, and the merging of designer and craftsman. Krenov was deeply influenced by his mentor, Swedish designer Carl Malmsten, who was himself enamored of the style and substance of English Arts and Crafts.

In addition to the thousands he reached through his writings, Krenov had a personal impact on hundreds more through the cabinetmaking program he headed from 1981 to 2002 at the College of the Redwoods in Fort Bragg, California. Krenov's affection for the English Arts and Crafts was evident at the school, where an obscure booklet of Barnsley's designs was a revered text.

Krenov called his unplanned method of furniture making a "fingertip adventure," echoing Ruskin's call for the designer and craftsman to be met in one man.

Arts and Crafts Revival

THE ARTS AND CRAFTS REVIVAL shows no sign of abating. Each year new makers appear. The following gallery of contemporary Arts and Crafts furniture makers and designers is by no means exhaustive. They represent a cross section of the revival.

DAVID BERMAN BUILT *and painted this replica of a Voysey shelf clock. The original was exhibited at the 1899 Arts and Crafts Exhibition in London. Berman paints the surfaces himself.*

DAVID BERMAN,
PLYMOUTH, MASSACHUSETTS

In 1982 David Berman found an extensive archive on the English Arts and Crafts architect C. F. A. Voysey. Looking through the material, Berman became enamored of Voysey's work, and he went on to do extensive research of his own.

Not content with merely reading about Voysey, Berman began building reproductions of Voysey's furniture. He also re-created Voysey designs for fabrics, wallpaper, and hardware. He made a series of light fixtures inspired by Voysey's pattern designs. Today much of Berman's time is devoted to work as a design consultant, but he balances that with hands-on work in his Plymouth studio.

DAVID BERMAN INCORPORATES *original Voysey pattern designs in new furniture. The "Mermaid" motif in the panels of this hanging lamp, sawn from sheet copper, is derived from a Voysey fabric.*

THIS HARVEY ELLIS-DESIGNED *music cabinet by Jeff Franke is in ebonized oak. The precisely crafted copper, pewter, and wood inlay on book-matched panels takes the Stickley style to the level of Greene and Greene craftsmanship.*

JEFF FRANKE, MINNEAPOLIS, MINNESOTA

In 1990, with a degree in fine arts and a successful graphic design business, Jeff Franke began collecting American Arts and Crafts antiques. Five years later, he opened Northern Craftsman Workshops.

Franke's work is so meticulous that his reproductions sometimes outdo the craftsmanship of the originals. He does all the inlay work himself. In addition to building reproductions, Franke designs new pieces in Gustav Stickley's style.

ANTIQUE GRUEBY TILE *that was salvaged from a fireplace gives Franke's Stickley-designed side table a double link to the Arts and Crafts period.*

DAVID B. HELLMAN, WATERTOWN, MASSACHUSETTS

David Hellman studied at the renowned two-year woodworking program at Boston's North Bennett Street School.

A former optometrist, he opened his furniture shop in 1992 and almost immediately focused his work on the designs of Greene and Greene. Hellman occasionally works in the styles of other Arts and Crafts designers but always returns to the Greene and Greene idiom, whether he is building replicas or new designs.

EXCEPT FOR ONE SMALL ITEM *of additional inlay, these two armchairs are reproductions by David Hellman of the 1907 Greene and Greene chairs for the Blacker House in Pasadena. They are mahogany with ebony, silver, purpleheart, and white oak inlay.*

HELLMANN'S SIDEBOARD *is a near copy of the one designed by Greene and Greene for their Thorsen House in Berkeley in 1909. Hellman shortened the design a few inches to suit his client's space. Built in mahogany it features inlays of ebony, abalone, mother-of-pearl, oak, and fruitwood.*

INSPIRED BY AN ORIGINAL *Harvey Ellis design, this secretary offers display space and book storage along with a drop-front desk.*

WARREN HILE,
MONROVIA, CALIFORNIA

Warren Hile's furniture career began unexpectedly. He was restoring an old bungalow and wanted to furnish it with pieces appropriate to the period. His first project was a Morris chair. As he built other pieces, a business was born.

Warren Hile Studio, which started with two people in 1991, now employs 30 skilled craftsmen. The shop employs traditional joinery and maintains a high standard of quality. Warren Hile Studio makes furniture in production and offers a wide range of American Arts and Crafts pieces.

WARREN HILE STUDIO'S *paneled settle employs the architectural detailing typical of furniture by Prairie School designers such as Frank Lloyd Wright.*

James Ipekjian, Pasadena, California

James Ipekjian started making furniture more than 30 years ago while employed as a modelmaker for the aerospace industry. In the early 1980s Ipekjian helped restore Charles and Henry Greene's Duncan-Irwin House .

Ipekjian's impeccable work led to commissions to replicate the original furniture for several Greene and Greene masterpieces, including the Blacker House. He also reproduced furniture for Frank Lloyd Wright's landmark Hollyhock House in Los Angeles.

James Ipekjian's reproduction *of Greene and Greene's Thorsen House armchair of 1909 is built in mahogany and ebony. The crest-rail inlay is white oak, satine, abalone, and rosewood. The original chairs were made in 1909 for the Thorsen House in Berkeley.*

STEPHEN LAMONT,
EAST TISTED, ENGLAND
Born in the United States, Stephen Lamont left the country—and a career in aviation—in 1986 to train with master furniture maker Christopher Faulkner in Devon, England. In 1996 he returned to join the storied Edward Barnsley Workshops in Hampshire. Lamont worked there for four years before opening his own shop in nearby East Tisted.

Lamont produces furniture inspired by the Cotswold tradition of his English mentors.

STEPHEN LAMONT'S DINING *chairs recall Ernest Gimson's armchairs for the Bedales School library. The table and chairs are made of oak.*

MICHAEL MCGLYNN, MINNEAPOLIS, MINNESOTA Michael McGlynn makes furniture in his Minneapolis shop that reflects a high regard for the Prairie School designers as well as the work of Greene and Greene, C. R. Mackintosh, and Josef Hoffmann. The Minneapolis Institute of Arts commissioned McGlynn to reproduce original furnishings for several houses designed by Prairie School architects William Purcell and George Elmslie.

MICHAEL MCGLYNN'S WHITE *oak side chair is a reproduction of the dining chair designed by George Grant Elmslie for the T. B. Keith House in Eau Claire, Wisconsin.*

BUILT OF CHERRY, *McGlynn's sideboard fuses Prairie-style vocabulary with Greene and Greene proportions.*

KEVIN P. RODEL, POWNAL, MAINE

Kevin Rodel taught himself wood-working, and in 1978, he took a job building Shaker furniture at Thos. Moser Cabinetmakers. In 1986, he and his wife, Susan Mack, opened their own shop, Mack & Rodel. Since discovering the Arts and Crafts revival in the late 1980s, they have been exploring the Arts and Crafts idiom exclusively.

Once a year, Rodel teaches a course on Arts and Crafts design at the School for Furniture Craftsmanship in Rockland, Maine.

KEVIN P. RODEL'S PRAIRIE DESK, *designed in 1993, was inspired mainly by Frank Lloyd Wright's residential architecture. This version is in cherry and black leather with ebony accents.*

THIS BOOKCASE *was inspired by Harvey Ellis's furniture for Stickley as well as by Glasgow Style metalwork and inlay. Built in cherry with maple and pewter inlay, it has copper pulls and panes of handblown glass.*

CHRISTOPHER VICKERS, FROME, ENGLAND

Christopher Vickers has been making furniture and wooden boxes since 1987. Vickers attended the London College of Furniture, and he has since served as a teacher there. His furniture is strongly influenced by the works of English Arts and Crafts designers C. F. A. Voysey, M. H. Baillie Scott, Philip Webb, and Ernest Gimson. In 2001 Vickers completed a commission to furnish the William Morris Room in the Hotel Pattee in Perry, Iowa.

CRISTOPHER VICKERS'S COTSWOLD *display cabinet, in English oak with bog oak and holly inlays, shows the influences of Ernest Gimson and Peter Waals.*

BUILT OF BROWN OAK AND CEDAR *with embossed leather panels, forged iron hinges, and copper repoussé panels inside the lid, this chest represents four of the crafts practiced by C. R. Ashbee's Guild of Handicraft. It was made to celebrate the centenary of the Guild's move from London to Chipping Campden in 1902.*

THIS TALL CHERRY CABINET *clearly displays a thorough control of line and proportion. The door-panel carvings depict California bay laurel.*

DEBEY ZITO,
SAN FRANCISCO, CALIFORNIA

Debey Zito has had her own shop in San Francisco for 25 years, where she builds furniture and teaches woodworking. Her interest began in high school. At San Diego State University, she majored in industrial design with a concentration in wood and metal.

Zito has long admired the pure, functional forms of Asian and Scandinavian furniture, and the oeuvre of Greene and Greene. Her work reflects European and English Arts and Crafts influences. Her partner, Terry Schmitt's carvings have become a signature of Zito's furniture.

HAMMERED COPPER TOP AND *drawer pulls by Bay Area coppersmith Audel Davis, embellish Debey Zito's walnut server. The carved panels of English peas were executed by Terry Schmitt.*

Selected Bibliography

Anscombe, Isabelle. *Arts & Crafts Style*. New York: Rizzoli Press, 1991.

The Art Institute of Chicago. *The Prairie School, Design Vision for the Midwest*. Chicago: The Art Institute of Chicago, 1995.

Arwas, Victor. *Art Nouveau: From Mackintosh to Liberty*. London: Andreas Papadakis Publisher, 2000.

Atterbury, Paul and Clive Wainwright. *Pugin: A Gothic Passion*. New Haven, CT: Yale University Press, 1994.

Baillie Scott, M. H. *Houses and Gardens: Arts & Crafts Interiors*. Reprinted. Suffolk, England: Antique Collectors Club, 1995.

Bartinique, A. Patricia. *Gustav Stickley: His Craft*. Parsippany, NJ: The Craftsman Farms Foundation, 1992.

Billcliffe, Roger. *Charles Rennie Mackintosh: The Complete Furniture, Furniture Drawings and Interior Designs*. London: John Murry Ltd., 1986.

Bowman, Leslie Greene. *American Arts & Crafts: Virtue in Design*. Boston: Los Angeles County Museum of Art and Bullfinch Press, 1990.

Brett, David. *C. R. Mackintosh: The Poetics of Workmanship*. London: Reaktion Books, 1992.

Burkhauser, Jude. *Glasgow Girls: Women in Art & Design 1880–1920*. Cape May, NJ: Red Ochre Press, 1993.

Carruthers, Annette. *Edward Barnsley and his Workshop: Arts and Crafts in the Twentieth Century*. Oxford: White Cockade Publishing, 1992.

Cathers, David and Alexander Vertikoff. *Stickley Style*. New York: Simon & Schuster, 1999.

Crawford, Alan. *Charles Rennie Mackintosh*. London: Thames & Hudson Ltd., 1995.

Cumming, Elizabeth and Wendy Kaplan. *The Arts & Crafts Movement*. London: Thames & Hudson Ltd., 1991.

D'Ambrosio, Anna Tobin. *The Distinction of Being Different: Joseph P. McHugh & the American Arts & Crafts Movement*. Utica, NY: Munson-Williams-Proctor Institute, 1994.

Davey, Peter. *Arts and Crafts Architecture*. London: Phaidon Press, 1995.

Davidoff, Donald A. and Robert L. Zarrow. *Early L. & J. G. Stickley Furniture*. New York: Dover Publications, 1992.

Davidoff, Donald A. and Stephen Gray. *Innovation and Derivation, the Contributions of L. & J. G. Stickley to the American Arts & Crafts Movement*. Parsippany, NJ: The Craftsman Farms Foundation, 1995.

Durant, Stuart. *C. F. A. Voysey*. New York: St. Martin's Press, 1992.

Fish, Marilyn. *Gustav Stickley: Heritage and Early Years*. North Caldwell, NJ: Little Pond Press, 1997.

Gere, Charlotte and Michael Whiteway. *Nineteenth Century Design: From Pugin to Mackintosh*. New York: Harry N. Abrams Inc., 1994.

Green, Nancy E. and Jessie Poesch. *Arthur Wesley Dow and American Arts & Crafts*. New York: Harry N. Abrams, 2000.

Greensted, Mary. *The Arts & Crafts Movement in the Cotswolds*. Gloucestershire, England: Alan Sutton Publishing, 1993.

Haigh, Diane. *Baillie Scott: The Artistic House*. London: Academy Editions, 1995.

Harvey, Charles and Jon Press. *William Morris: Design and Enterprise in Victorian England*. Manchester, UK: Manchester University Press, 1991.

Heinz, Thomas A. *Frank Lloyd Wright: Interiors and Furniture*. London: Academy Editions, 1994.

Hitchmough, Wendy. *C. F. A. Voysey*. London: Phaidon, 1995.

Hitchmough, Wendy. *The Arts & Crafts Lifestyle and Design*. New York: Watson-Guptill Publishers, 2000.

Hosley, William. *The Japan Idea*. Hartford, CT: Wadsworth Athenaeum, 1990.

James, Michael L. *Drama in Design, The Life and Craft of Charles Rohlfs*. Buffalo, NY: Buffalo State College, 1994.

Kaplan, Wendy. *Leading "The Simple Life": The Arts and Crafts Movement in Britain, 1880-1910*. Miami Beach, FL: The Wolfsonian—Florida International University, 1999.

Kardon, Janet. *The Ideal Home: The History of the Twentieth-Century American Craft, 1900-1920*. New York: Harry N. Abrams, 1993.

Larkin, David and Bruce Brooks Pfeiffer. *Frank Lloyd Wright: The Masterworks*. New York: Rizzoli Press, 1993.

Lind, Carla. *The Wright Style*. New York: Archetype Press, 1992.

Lucie-Smith, Edward. *Furniture: A Concise History*. London: Thames and Hudson, 1993.

Mayer, Barbara. *In the Arts & Crafts Style*. San Francisco: Chronicle Books, 1992.

Moon, Karen. *George Walton: Designer and Architect*. Oxford: White Cockade Publishers, 1993.

New York School of Interior Design. *Four Studies on Charles Rennie Mackintosh*. New York: New York School of Interior Design, 1996.

O'Gorman, James F. *Three American Architects: Richardson, Sullivan and Wright, 1865–1915*. Chicago: University of Chicago Press, 1991.

Olivarez, Jennifer Komar. *Progressive Design in the Midwest*. Minneapolis: The Minneapolis Institute of Arts, 2000.

Roberts-Jones, Phillippe. *Brussels: Fin de Siecle*. Paris: Evergreen, 1999.

Robertson, Cheryl. *Frank Lloyd Wright and George Mann Niedecken: Prairie School Collaborators*. Milwaukee: Milwaukee Art Museum and Museum of Our National Heritage, 1999.

Sanders, Barry. *A Complex Fate: Gustav Stickley and the Craftsman Movement*. New York: Preservation Press, 1996.

Sangl, Sigrid. *Biedermeier to Bauhaus*. New York: Harry N. Abrams, 2001.

Smith, Bruce and Alexander Vertikoff. *Greene & Greene: Masterworks*. San Francisco: Chronicle Books, 1998.

Thomas, George E. *William L. Price: Arts & Crafts to Modern Design*. New York: Princeton Architectural Press, 2000.

Trapp, Kenneth R. *The Arts & Crafts Movement in California: Living the Good Life*. New York: Abbeville Press, 1993.

Turgeon, Kitty and Robert Rust. *The Roycroft Campus*. Charleston, SC: Arcadia Publishers, 1999.

Turn of the Century Publishers. *Quaint Furniture in Arts & Crafts*. Stickley Brothers catalog reprint. New York: Turn of the Century Publishers, 1988.

Via, Marie and Marjorie B. Searl. *Head, Heart and Hand: Elbert Hubbard and the Roycrofters*. Rochester, NY: University of Rochester Press, 1994.

Wilhide, Elizabeth. *William Morris: Décor and Design*. New York: Harry N. Abrams, 1991.

Resources

Contemporary Furniture Makers in the Arts and Crafts Tradition

The Edward Barnsley Workshop
Cockshott Ln., Froxfield
Petersfield
Hampshire, GU32 1BB, U.K.
44 (0) 1730 827233

David Berman
P. O. Box 1109
Plymouth, MA 02362
(508) 746-1847

Dennis Bertucci
P. O. Box 91
Walton, NY 13856
(607) 865-8372

Black Swamp Handcraft
2711 Albon Rd.
Maumee, OH 43537
(419) 861-3601
cmoremac@aol.com

Todd Brotherton
P. O. Box 404
Mt. Shasta, CA 96067
(530) 938-4000
todd@snowcrest.net

Catskill Furnituremakers
11 Field Ct.
Kingston, NY 12401
(845) 339-8029
www.catskillfurniture.com

Claybaugh Studios
852 E. Hutchenson
Pittsburgh, PA 15218
(412) 247-5442
www.claybaughstudios.com

Arnold d'Epagnier
14201 Notley Rd.
Colesville, MD 20904
(301) 384-1663

Dryad Studios
478 CR 9590
Green Forest, AR 72638
(870) 553-2251
www.dryadstudios.com

John Reed Fox
179 Pope Rd.
Acton, MA 01720
(978) 635-0807

Jeff Franke
P. O. Box 19558
Minneapolis, MN 55419
(612) 824-6290

Green Design Furniture Co.
267 Commercial St.
Portland, ME 04101
(800) 853-4234

Erik Hanson
1406 Granda Ave.
San Diego, CA 92102
(619) 239-6150
www.irvinggill.com

David Hellman
P. O. Box 526
Watertown, MA 02471-0526
(617) 923-4829
www.dbhellman.com

Warren Hile Studio
1823 Enterprise Way
Monrovia, CA 91016
(626) 355-4382

Holton Furniture & Frame
5515 Doyle St. #2
Emeryville, CA 94608
(800) 250-5277

James Ipekjian
768 N. Fair Oaks Ave.
Pasadena, CA 91103
(626) 792-5025

Paul Kemner
2829 Rockwood
Toledo, OH 43610
(419) 241-8278
pkemner@bright.net

Stephen Lamont
Rotherfield Estate
East Tisted
Hants. GU34 3RT, U.K.
(0)142 058-8362

M. T. Maxwell Furniture Co.
715 Liberty St.
Bedford, VA 24523
(800) 686-1844
www.maxwellfurniture.com

John McAlevey
Ridge Rd.
HCR 35 Box 668
Tenants Harbor, ME 04860
(207) 372-6455
jmcalevey@ctel.net

Tom McFadden
P. O. Box 162
Philo, CA 95466
(707) 895-3606

Michael McGlynn
501 First Ave. N.
Minneapolis, MN 55413
(612) 331-1739

Whit McLeod
P. O. Box 132
Arcata, CA 95518
(707) 822-7307

Thomas Pafk
1054 Olean Rd.
East Aurora, NY 14052
(716) 655-3229
www.thomaspafkdesign.com

Darrell Peart Furnituremaker
3419 C St. NE #16
Auburn, WA 98002
(425) 277-4070
www.furnituremaker.com

Prairie School Interiors
496 Rose Ln.
Bartlett, IL 60103
(630) 837-2653
www.prairie-school.com

Michael Pulhalski
1526 First Ave. S.
Seattle, WA 98134
(206) 233-9581

Rocky Coast Joinery
830 Hope Rd.
Camden, ME 04843
(207) 763-4770
info@rockycoastjoinery.com

Kevin P. Rodel
44 Leighton Rd.
Pownal, ME 04069
(207) 688-4483
macrodel@aol.com
www.neaguild.com/macrodel

L. & J. G. Stickley
P. O. Box 480
Manlius, NY 13104
(315) 682-5500
www.stickley.com

Thomas Stangeland
309 8th Ave. N.
Seattle, WA 98109
(206) 622-2004
www.artestcraftsman.net

Thomas S. Stockton
P. O. Box 38
Montgomery Creek, CA 96065
(530) 337-6797
www.dnai.com/~starbuck

Swartzendruber Hardwood Creations
1100 Chicago Ave.
Goshen, IL 46526
(800) 531-2502

Christopher Vickers
24 Portway, Frome
Somerset BA11 1QT, U.K.
(0)137 346-7897
www.ArtsandCraftsDesigns.com

Voorhees Craftsman
P. O. Box 1938
Rohnert Park, CA 94927
(888) 982-6377

Debey Zito
55 Bronte St.
San Francisco, CA 94110
(415) 648-6861

Antique Dealers and Contemporary Retailers

John Alexander Ltd.
10 W. Gravers Ln.
Philadelphia, PA 19118
(215) 242-0741
www.johnalexanderltd.com

H. Blairman & Sons, Ltd.
119 Mount St.
London, W1Y 5HB, U.K.
44 (0) 207 493 0444
blairman@atlas.co.uk

Circa 1910 Antiques
7206 Melrose Ave.
Hollywood, CA 90046
(323) 965-1910
www.circa1900antiques.com

The Craftsman Home
3048 Claremont Ave.
Berkeley, CA 94705
(510) 655-6503
www.craftsmanhome.com

Dalton's Decorative Antiques
1931 James St.
Syracuse, NY 13206
(315) 463-1568
www.daltons.com

Michael Fitzsimmons Decorative Arts
311 W. Superior St.
Chicago, IL 60610
(312) 787-0496
www.fitzdecarts.com

Gallery 532
142 Duane St.
New York, NY 10013
(212) 219-1327
www.gallery532.com

Mark Golding
The Arts & Crafts Home
25A Clifton Terrace Brighton
Sussex BN1 3HA, U.K.
(0)127 332-7774
www.achome.co.uk

Historical Designs Inc.
306 E. 61st St.
New York, NY 10021
(212) 593-4528
www.historicaldesign.com

House of Orange
Alameda, CA 94501
(510) 523-3378

Jeffrey's Royal Oak
404 E. 4th St.
Royal Oak, MI 48067
www.jeffreyclay.com

JMW Gallery
144 Lincoln St.
Boston, MA 02111
www.jmwgallery.com

Isak Lindenauer Antiques
4143 19th St.
San Francisco, CA 94114
(415) 552-6436

Don Marek
Heartwood
956 Cherry St.
Grand Rapids, MI 49506
(616) 454-1478

Peter-Roberts Antiques, Inc.
39 Bond St.
New York, NY 10012
(212) 477-9690
pra.nyc@verizon.net

John Toomey Gallery
818 N. Blvd.
Oak Park, IL 60301
(708) 383-5234
www.treadwaygallery.com

Places to Visit

UNITED STATES

Bryn Athyn Cathedral
1000 Cathedral Rd.
Bryn Athyn, PA 19009
(215) 947-0266

Craftsman Farms
(Gustav Stickley's home)
2352 Rte. 10 West, #5
Morris Plains, NJ 07950
(973) 540-1165
www.parsippany.net/craftsman-farms

*Fonthill, Moravian Pottery &
Tile Works, and the Mercer Museum*
(Henry Chapman Mercer's
house and workshop)
84 S. Pine St.
Doylestown, PA 18901
(215) 348-9461
www.mercermuseum.org

Frank Lloyd Wright Home and Studio
951 Chicago Ave.
Oak Park, IL 60302
(708) 848-1976

The Gamble House and Bookstore
4 Westmoreland St.
Pasadena, CA 91103
(626) 793-3334
www.gamblehouse.org

Pleasant Home
(Designed by George W. Maher)
217 Home Ave.
Oak Park, IL 60302
(708) 383-2654
www.oprf.com/phf

Purcell-Cutts House
(Designed by Purcell & Elmslie)
2328 Lake Pl.
Minneapolis, MN 55403
(612) 870-3131
www.artsmia.org/unified-vision

Roycroft Museum
363 Oakwood Ave.
East Aurora, NY 14052
(716) 652-4735
www.roycrofter.com/museum

UNITED KINGDOM

Blackwell
(House by M. H. Baillie Scott)
Bowness-on-Windermere
Cumbria LA23 3JR, U.K.
44 (0) 153 944 6139
www.blackwell.org.uk

Broad Leys
(C. F. A. Voysey house)
Ghyll Head, Windermere
Cumbria LA23 3LJ, U.K.
44 (0) 153 944 3284
www.voysey-broadleys.com

Cheltenham Art Gallery and Museums
(Cotswold Arts and Crafts
furniture)
Clarence St.
Cheltenham GL50 3JT, U.K.
44 (0) 1242 237431
www.artsandcraftsmuseum.org.uk

Glasgow School of Art
167 Renfrew St.
Glasgow G3 6RQ, Scotland
44 (0) 141 353 4526
www.gsa.ac.uk/mackintosh

Hill House
(Mackintosh house)
Upper Colquhoun St.
Helensburgh G84 9AJ, UK
44 (0) 143 667 3900
www.nts.org.uk/hillhouse

Kelmscott Manor
Kelmscott
Lechlade, Gloucestershire G17
3HJ, U.K.
44 (0) 136 725 2486
www.kelmscottmanor.co.uk

Hunterian Museum and Art Gallery
University of Glasgow
Glasgow G12 8QQ, Scotland
44 (0) 141 330 4221
www.hunterian.gla.ac.uk

Rodmarton Manor
(Designed by Ernest Barnsley)
Cirencester
Gloucestershire GL7 6PF, UK
44 (0) 128 584 1253
www.rodmarton-manor.co.uk

Standen
(Philip Webb house)
East Grinstead
Sussex RH19 4NE, U.K.
44 (0) 134 232 3029
www.nationaltrust.org.uk/places
/standen; www.vam.ac.uk

Credits

p. v: Courtesy David Rago Auctions Inc. © 2002

p. vi: (left) Photo © Rick Echelmeyer, courtesy Robert Edwards; (bottom) © The Fine Art Society

p. 1: © V & A Picture Library, Victoria and Albert Museum

p. 2: Photo by Jonathan Binzen

Chapter 1

p. 4: Courtesy Meredith W. Mendes & Michael Levitin, Photo by Randy O'Rourke

p. 6: Photo by Jonathan Binzen

p. 7: © V & A Picture Library, Victoria and Albert Museum

p. 8: (bottom left) Photo by Jonathan Binzen

p. 9: Courtesy The Gamble House, USC, Photo by Randy O'Rourke

p. 10: Courtesy L. & J. G. Stickley Co., Photo by Randy O'Rourke

p. 11: (top) Courtesy H. Blairman & Sons, Ltd.; (bottom) © V & A Picture Library, Victoria and Albert Museum

p. 12: (top) Courtesy Crab Tree Farm, Lake Bluff, Illinois, Photo by Randy O'Rourke; (bottom) (Photo by Jonathan Binzen

p. 13: (top) Courtesy private collection, Photo by Randy O'Rourke; (bottom) © Glasgow Museums: Art Gallery & Museum, Kelvingrove; George Logan (E1896.52)

p. 14: (top) Courtesy Van Andle Museum

p. 14: (bottom) Courtesy Belle E. and Alexander Moser, Photo by Randy O'Rourke

p. 15: (top) Courtesy Hunterian Art Gallery; (bottom) Photo by Jonathan Binzen

p. 16: (top) Photo by Jonathan Binzen; (bottom) © V & A Picture Library, Victoria and Albert Museum

p. 17: (top) Courtesy private collection, Photo by Randy O'Rourke; Courtesy David Rago Auctions Inc. © 2002

Chapter 2

p. 18: © Fine Arts Society

p. 20: (top) © V & A Picture Library, Victoria and Albert Museum; (bottom) © V & A Picture Library, Victoria and Albert Museum

p. 21: (bottom) Courtesy H. Blairman & Sons, Ltd.

p. 22: (top) © V & A Picture Library, Victoria and Albert Museum; (bottom) Private collection/Bridgeman Art Library

p. 23: Courtesy J.R. Burrows

p. 24: © V & A Picture Library, Victoria and Albert Museum

p. 25: Courtesy H. Blairman & Sons, Ltd.

p. 26: © Cheltenham Art Gallery & Museums, Gloucestershire, UK/Bridgeman Art Library

p. 27: (top) © V & A Picture Library, Victoria and Albert Museum; (bottom) © The Delaware Art Museum. acquired through the bequest of Doris Wright Anderson and the F.V. duPont Acquisition Fund, 1997

p. 28: Courtesy H. Blairman & Sons, Ltd.

p. 29: Courtesy H. Blairman & Sons, Ltd.

p. 30: © V & A Picture Library, Victoria and Albert Museum

p. 31: © Cheltenham Art Gallery & Museums, Gloucestershire, UK/Bridgeman Art Library

Chapter 3

p. 32: Photo by Jonathan Binzen

p. 35: (top) © Cheltenham Art Gallery & Museums, Gloucestershire, UK/Bridgeman Art Library; (bottom) © Cheltenham Art Gallery & Museum Service

p. 36: (top) Photo by Jonathan Binzen; (bottom) Photo by Jonathan Binzen

p. 37: (top) Photo by Jonathan Binzen; (bottom) Photo by Jonathan Binzen

p. 38: (top) © Cheltenham Art Gallery & Museums, Gloucestershire, UK/Bridgeman Art Library; (bottom) © Cheltenham Art Gallery & Museums, Gloucestershire, UK/Bridgeman Art Library

p. 39: (top) © Randy O'Rourke; (bottom) © V & A Picture Library, Victoria and Albert Museum

p. 40: © V & A Picture Library, Victoria and Albert Museum

p. 41: © V & A Picture Library, Victoria and Albert Museum

p. 42: © Cheltenham Art Gallery & Museums, Gloucestershire, UK/Bridgeman Art Library

p. 43: (top) Photo by Jonathan Binzen; (bottom) © Cheltenham Art Gallery & Museums, Gloucestershire, UK/Bridgeman Art Library

p. 44: © Cheltenham Art Gallery & Museums, Gloucestershire, UK/Bridgeman Art Library

p. 45: (top) Courtesy H. Blairman & Sons, Ltd.; (bottom) Courtesy H. Blairman & Sons, Ltd.

Chapter 4

p. 46: Courtesy Andre and Ann Chaves, Photo by Randy O'Rourke

p. 48: (top) © William Morris Gallery, Walthamstow, UK/Bridgeman Art Library; (bottom) © V & A Picture Library, Victoria and Albert Museum

p. 49: Photo by Jonathan Binzen

p. 50: © The Fine Art Society, London, UK/Bridgeman Art Library

p. 51: (top) Courtesy The Studio, 1904; (bottom) © Private Collection/The Fine Art Society, London, UK/Bridgeman Art Library

p. 52: (left) Photo by Jonathan Binzen; (right) Photo courtesy The Studio, 1899

p. 53: © Randy O'Rourke

p. 54: (top) © Fine Arts Society; (bottom) Photo by Jonathan Binzen

p. 55: Courtesy David Rudd and Debbie Goldwein Rudd, Photo by Randy O'Rourke

p. 56: (top) Courtesy Crab Tree Farm, Lake Bluff, Illinois, Photo by Randy O'Rourke; (bottom) © V & A Picture Library, Victoria and Albert Museum

p. 57: Los Angeles County Museum of Art, Gift of Max Palevsky, Photograph © 2003 Museum Associates/LACMA

p. 58: (top) © V & A Picture Library, Victoria and Albert Museum; (bottom) © Private Collection/The Fine Art Society, London, UK/Bridgeman Art Library

p. 59: (left and right) Courtesy H. Blairman & Sons, Ltd.

p. 60: (top) Courtesy John and Karen Baca, Decorative Arts, Chicago, Photo by Randy O'Rourke; (middle) Courtesy Fitzsimmons Decorative Arts, Chicago, Photo by Randy O'Rourke; (bottom) Courtesy H. Blairman & Sons, Ltd.

p. 61: (top and bottom) © Fine Arts Society

Chapter 5

p. 62: Courtesy The Hunterian Museum and Art

p. 64: © Glasgow School of Art

p. 65: (top) © Glasgow School of Art

p. 65: (bottom) © Private Collection/ The Fine Art Society, London, UK/Bridgeman Art Library

p. 66: (top) Courtesy Studio Yearbook, 1907; (bottom) © Glasgow School of Art

p. 67: (top) © The Hunterian Museum and Art Gallery, University of Glasgow, Mackintosh Collection; (bottom) © Glasgow School of Art

p. 68: © Glasgow School of Art

p. 69: (left) © Glasgow Museums: Art Gallery & Museum, Kelvingrove; George Walton, The Lovat toilet table 1900 (E1982.38)

p. 70: (top) © Glasgow Museums: Art Gallery & Museum, Kelvingrove; E.A. Taylor design for Ingleneuk 1902 (E1982.77.4); (bottom) Courtesy John Alexander, Ltd., Photo by Randy O'Rourke

p. 71: (top) © Glasgow Museums: Art Gallery & Museum, Kelvingrove; E.A. Taylor (E1976.14); (bottom left and right) © Glasgow School of Art

p. 72: (left and right) Courtesy H. Blairman & Sons, Ltd.

p. 73: (top) © Glasgow Museums: Art Gallery & Museum, Kelvingrove; George Walton, the Holland Cabinet (E1995.14); (bottom) © Randy O'Rourke

p. 74: © Glasgow Museums: Art Gallery & Museum, Kelvingrove; E.A. Taylor (E1976.19)

p. 75: (top) © Glasgow Museums: Art Gallery & Museum, Kelvingrove; E.A. Taylor (E1981.126); (bottom left and right) © Randy O'Rourke

p. 75: (bottom right) Courtesy John Alexander, Ltd., Photo by Randy O'Rourke

p. 76: (bottom) © Glasgow Museums: Art Gallery & Museum, Kelvingrove; George Logan (E1896.52)

p. 77: (top) © Glasgow Museums: Art Gallery & Museum, Kelvingrove; George Logan 1901 (E1984.137), (bottom) © Glasgow Museums: Art Gallery & Museum, Kelvingrove; John Ednie (E1988.111.4)

p. 78: (top, bottom left and right) © The Hunterian Museum and Art Gallery, University of Glasgow, Mackintosh Collection

p. 79: © Glasgow School of Art

p. 80: All photos © Glasgow School of Art

p. 81: © The Hunterian Museum and Art Gallery, University of Glasgow, Mackintosh Collection

Chapter 6

p. 85: (bottom) © V & A Picture Library, Victoria and Albert Museum

p. 86: (bottom) © V & A Picture Library, Victoria and Albert Museum

p. 87: (top) © V & A Picture Library, Victoria and Albert Museum

p. 89: © H. Blairman & Sons, Ltd.

p. 90: Courtesy David Rago Auctions Inc. © 2002

p. 92: © V & A Picture Library, Victoria and Albert Museum

p. 93: © V & A Picture Library, Victoria and Albert Museum

Chapter 7

p. 94: Courtesy Crab Tree Farm, Lake Bluff, Illinois, Photo by Randy O'Rourke

p. 96: Photos © Collection of Stickley furniture, Courtesy of Mr. & Mrs. Alfred Audi, Photography by Randy O'Rourke

p. 97: (bottom) © Private collection, Photo by Randy O'Rourke

p. 98: Courtesy David rudd and Debbie Goldwein Rudd, Photo by Randy O'Rourke

p. 99: (bottom) Courtesy Deborah and Dennis Conta, Photo by Randy O'Rourke

p. 100: (top and right) Courtesy L. & J. G. Stickley, Photo by Randy O'Rourke; (bottom) © Glasgow School of Art

p. 101: Courtesy David Rudd and Debbie Goldwein Rudd, Photo by Randy O'Rourke

p. 102: (top) Photo © Rich Echelmeyer, Courtesy Robert Edwards; (bottom) Courtesy Crab Tree Farm, Lake Bluff, Illinois, Photo by Randy O'Rourke

p. 103: (top) Photo by Jonathan Binzen; (bottom) Courtesy Crab Tree Farm, Lake Bluff, Illinois, Photo by Randy O'Rourke

p. 104: (top) Courtesy David Rago Auctions Inc. © 2002; (bottom) Photo © Rich Echelmeyer, Courtesy Robert Edwards

p. 105: Courtesy David Rago Auctions Inc. © 2002

p. 106: (left) Courtesy L. & J. G. Stickley, Photo by Randy O'Rourke; (right) Courtesy David Rago Auctions Inc. © 2002

p. 107: © Collection of Stickley furniture, Courtesy of Mr. & Mrs. Alfred Audi, Photography by Randy O'Rourke

p. 108: Courtesy David Rudd and Debbie Goldwein Rudd, Photo by Randy O'Rourke; (bottom) © Private collection, Photo by Randy O'Rourke

p. 109: (top) Courtesy David Rudd and Debbie Goldwein Rudd, Photo by Randy O'Rourke; (bottom) © Private collection, Photo by Randy O'Rourke

p. 110: Courtesy David Rudd and Debbie Goldwein Rudd, Photo by Randy O'Rourke

p. 111: (top) Courtesy David Rudd and Debbie Goldwein Rudd, Photo by Randy O'Rourke; (bottom) Courtesy David Rudd and Debbie Goldwein Rudd, Photo by Randy O'Rourke

p. 112: © Collection of Stickley furniture, Courtesy of Mr. & Mrs. Alfred Audi, Photography by Randy O'Rourke

p. 113: © Collection of Stickley furniture, Courtesy of Mr. & Mrs. Alfred Audi, Photography by Randy O'Rourke

p. 114: (top) Courtesy Deborah and Dennis Conta, Photo by Randy O'Rourke; (bottom left and right) © Collection of Stickley furniture, Courtesy of Mr. & Mrs. Alfred Audi, Photography by Randy O'Rourke

p. 115: (top) Photo © Rick Echelmeyer, Courtesy Robert Edwards; (bottom) Courtesy David Rago Auctions Inc. © 2002

p. 116: (top) Courtesy David Rago Auctions Inc. © 2002; (bottom) Courtesy David Rago Auctions Inc. © 2002

p. 118: (top) Courtesy Van Andle Museum; (bottom) Courtesy Van Andle Museum

p. 119: (top) Courtesy David Rago Auctions Inc. © 2002; (bottom) Courtesy David Rago Auctions Inc. © 2002

Chapter 8

p. 120: Courtesy Meredith W. Mendes and Michael Levitin, Photo by Randy O'Rourke

p. 122: Courtesy Van Andle Museum

p. 123: (top) Courtesy Van Andle Museum; (bottom) Courtesy Van Andle Museum

p. 124: (top left) Courtesy Van Andle Museum; (top right) Courtesy Van Andle Museum; (bottom left) Courtesy Van Andle Museum

p. 126: © Private collection, Photo by Randy O'Rourke

p. 127: Courtesy Meredith W. Mendes and Michael Levitin, Photo by Randy O'Rourke

p. 129: (top left) Courtesy of Craftsman Auctions; (top right) © Glasgow School of Art; (bottom) Courtesy of Craftsman Auctions

p. 130: (top) Courtesy of Craftsman Auctions; (bottom) Courtesy Fitzsimmons Decorative Arts, Chicago, Photo by Randy O'Rourke

p. 131: Courtesy Swedenborgian Church, San Francisco, Photo by Randy O'Rourke

p. 132: (top) Courtesy Swedenborgian Church, San Francisco, Photo by Randy O'Rourke

p. 134: Courtesy Van Andle Museum

p. 135: (top) Courtesy Van Andle Museum, Photo by Randy O'Rourke; (bottom) Courtesy Van Andle Museum, Photo by Randy O'Rourke

p. 136: (top) Courtesy of Craftsman Auctions; (bottom) Courtesy Van Andle Museum

p. 137: (top) Courtesy Van Andle Museum, Photo by Randy O'Rourke; (bottom) Courtesy Deborah and Dennis Conta, Photo by Randy O'Rourke

p. 138: (top) Courtesy Robert Edwards, Photo by Randy O'Rourke; (bottom) © Private collection, Photo by Randy O'Rourke

p. 139: (top) © Private collection, Photo by Randy O'Rourke; (bottom) Courtesy Van Andle Museum

p. 140: (top) Courtesy of Craftsman Auctions Inc.; (bottom) Photo by Rick Echelmeyer, Courtesy Robert Edwards

p. 141: (top) Courtesy Belle E. and Alexander Moser, Photo by Randy O'Rourke; (bottom) © Private collection, Photo by Randy O'Rourke

Chapter 9

p. 142: The Delaware Art Museum. Acquired through the bequest of Doris Wright Anderson and the F.V. duPont Acquisition Fund, 1997

p. 146: Courtesy Frank Lloyd Wright Home and Studio Foundation, Photo by Randy O'Rourke

p. 147: The Delaware Art Museum. Acquired through the bequest of Doris Wright Anderson and the F.V. duPont Acquisition Fund, 1997

p. 148: Frank Lloyd Wright portrait, ca. 1890–1895. Photographer: unknown. Courtesy of the Frank Lloyd Wright Preservation Trust. H&S H 177

p. 149: (top) Adam J. Mayer Residence, Courtesy Drs. David Stowe and Gene Webb, Photo by Randy O'Rourke; (bottom) Courtesy David Rags Auctions, Inc. © 2002

p. 150: Photo by Rick Echelmeyer, Courtesy Robert Edwards

p. 151: (top) Courtesy Pleasant Home Foundation, Oak Park, Illinois, Photo by Randy O'Rourke; (bottom) Courtesy John and Karen Baca, Photo by Randy O'Rourke

p. 152: Courtesy Frank Lloyd Wright Home and Studio Foundation, Photo by Randy O'Rourke

p. 154: Courtesy Meredith W. Mendes and Michael Levitin, Photo by Randy O'Rourke

p. 156: Adam J. Mayer Residence, Courtesy Drs. David Stowe and Gene Webb, Photo by Randy O'Rourke

p. 157: Adam J. Mayer Residence, Courtesy Drs. David Stowe and Gene Webb, Photo by Randy O'Rourke

p. 158: (top) Photo by Rick Echelmeyer, Courtesy Robert Edwards; (bottom) Photo by Rick Echelmeyer, Courtesy Robert Edwards

p. 159: Courtesy Pleasant Home Foundation, Photo by Randy O'Rourke

Chapter 10

p. 162: Courtesy Andre and Ann Chaves, Photo by Randy O'Rourke

p. 164: Photo by Rick Echelmeyer, Courtesy Robert Edwards

p. 165: (top) Photo by Rick Echelmeyer, Courtesy Robert Edwards; (bottom) Photo by Rick Echelmeyer, Courtesy Robert Edwards

p. 166: (top) Photo by Rick Echelmeyer, Courtesy Robert Edwards; (middle) Photo by Rick Echelmeyer, Courtesy Robert Edwards

p. 167: (bottom) Photo © Bruce Smith

p. 168: (left) Photo © Bruce Smith; (right) Photo by Jonathan Binzen; (top) Courtesy Roycroft Arts Museum, Boice Lydell, Photo by Randy O'Rourke; (bottom) Courtesy Kevin P. Rodel

p. 169: (top) Photo by Jonathan Binzen

p. 169: (bottom) Courtesy Elbert Hubbard-Roycroft Museum

p. 170: (top) Courtesy Elbert Hubbard-Roycroft Museum; (bottom) Courtesy Roycroft Arts Museum, Boice Lydell, Photo by Randy O'Rourke

p. 171: (top) Courtesy Roycroft Arts Museum, Boice Lydell, Photo by Randy O'Rourke

p. 171: (bottom left) Courtesy Roycroft Arts Museum, Boice Lydell, Photo by Randy O'Rourke; (bottom right) Courtesy Elbert Hubbard-Roycroft Museum, Photo by Randy O'Rourke

p. 172: (left) Courtesy David Rago Auctions, Inc., © 2002; (right) Courtesy Roycroft Arts Museum, Boice Lydell, Photo by Randy O'Rourke

p. 173: Courtesy Andre and Ann Chaves, Photo by Randy O'Rourke

p. 174: (top) Courtesy Robert Edwards, Photo by Randy O'Rourke; (bottom) © Private collection, Photo by Randy O'Rourke

p. 175: (left) Photos by Rick Echelmeyer, Courtesy Robert Edwards; (middle) Courtesy Bryn Athyn Cathedral, Photo by Randy O'Rourke; (right) Courtesy Bryn Athyn Cathedral, Photo by Randy O'Rourke

p. 177: (top and bottom right) Courtesy Bruce Smith; (bottom left) Courtesy Robert Edwards, Photo by Randy O'Rourke

p. 178: (left) Photo by Rick Echelmeyer, Courtesy Robert Edwards; (right) Photo by Rick Echelmeyer, Courtesy Robert Edwards

p. 179: (left) Courtesy Robert Edwards, Photo by Randy O'Rourke; (right) Courtesy Robert Edwards, Photo by Randy O'Rourke

p. 180: Courtesy Robert Edwards, Photo by Randy O'Rourke

p. 181: Photo by Rick Echelmeyer, Courtesy Robert Edwards

p. 182: (left) Courtesy Roycroft Arts Museum, Boice Lydell, Photo by Randy O'Rourke; (right) Courtesy Roycroft Arts Museum, Boice Lydell, Photo by Randy O'Rourke

p. 183: (top) Courtesy Andre and Ann Chaves, Photo by Randy O'Rourke; (bottom) Courtesy Elbert Hubbard-Roycroft Museum, Photo by Randy O'Rourke

p. 184: (left) Photo by Rick Echelmeyer, Courtesy Robert Edwards; (right) Photo by Rick Echelmeyer, Courtesy Robert Edwards

p. 185: (top) © Private collection, Photo by Randy O'Rourke

p. 185: (bottom) Photo by Rick Echelmeyer, Courtesy Robert Edwards

Chapter 11

p. 186: Courtesy The Gamble House, USC, Photo by Randy O'Rourke

p. 188: © Private collection, Photo by Randy O'Rourke

p. 189: © Private collection, Photo by Randy O'Rourke

p. 190: (top) © Private collection, Photo by Randy O'Rourke; (bottom) Courtesy David Rago Auctions, Inc., © 2002

p. 191: Courtesy Town of Clarence, New York, Historical Society, Photo by Randy O'Rourke

p. 192: (top) Photo by Rick Echelmeyer, Courtesy Robert Edwards; p. 192: (bottom) Private collection/Bridgeman Art Gallery

p. 193: (top) Photo by Rick Echelmeyer, Courtesy Robert Edwards

p. 195: Courtesy The Gamble House, USC, Photo by Randy O'Rourke

p. 197: Photo by Rick Echelmeyer, Courtesy Robert Edwards

p. 198: (top left) Courtesy The Gamble House, USC, Photo by Randy O'Rourke; (right) © Private collection, Photo by Randy O'Rourke

p. 199: (left) Courtesy Erik D. Hanson, Photo by Randy O'Rourke

p. 200: (left) Courtesy David Rago Auctions, Inc., © 2002; (right) © Private collection, Photo by Randy O'Rourke

p. 201: (left) © Private collection, Photo by Randy O'Rourke; (right) © Private collection, Photo by Randy O'Rourke; (right) © Private collection, Photo by Randy O'Rourke

p. 204: (left) Courtesy The Gamble House, USC, Photo by Randy O'Rourke; (right) Courtesy The Gamble House, USC, Photo by Randy O'Rourke

p. 205: Courtesy Randell Makinson, Photo by Thomas Heinz

Chapter 12

p. 206: Courtesy Kevin P. Rodel, Photo by Dennis Griggs

p. 208: Photo by Jonathan Binzen

p. 209: (left) Photo by Jonathan Binzen; (right) Photo by Jonathan Binzen

p. 210: (left) Photo by Jonathan Binzen

p. 211: (top) Photo by Jonathan Binzen; (bottom) Courtesy Wright, Photo by Brian Franczyk Photography

p. 212: (left) Photo by Jonathan Binzen; (right) Photo by Jonathan Binzen

p. 213: Photo by Jonathan Binzen

p. 214: Photo by Jonathan Binzen

p. 215: Photo by Jonathan Binzen

p. 216: (top) Courtesy David Berman, Photo by Randy O'Rourke; (bottom) Courtesy David Berman, Photo by Randy O'Rourke

p. 217: (top) Courtesy Jeff Franke, Northern Craftsman Workshops; (bottom) Courtesy Jeff Franke, Northern Craftsman Workshops

p. 218: (top) Courtesy David B. Hellman; (bottom) Courtesy David B. Hellman

p. 219: (top) © Photography by Alexander Vertikoff; (bottom) © Photography by Alexander Vertikoff

p. 220: (top) Courtesy James Ipekjian, photos by Randy O'Rourke; (bottom) Courtesy James Ipekjian, photos by Randy O'Rourke

p. 221: Courtesy Mr. and Mrs. Dominic Carney, Photo by Ian Parker

p. 222: (top) Courtesy Michael McGlynn; (bottom) Courtesy Michael McGlynn

p. 223: (top) Courtesy Kevin P. Rodel, Photo by Dennis Griggs; (bottom) Courtesy Kevin P. Rodel, Photo by Dennis Griggs

p. 224: (top) Courtesy Christopher Vickers, Photo by Daryl T. Enever; (bottom) Courtesy Christopher Vickers, Photo by Daryl T. Enever

p. 225: (top) Courtesy Chase Ewald, Photo by Randy O'Rourke

p. 225: (bottom) Courtesy Debey Zito, Photo by Richard Sargent

Index